FORECASTING
FOR
MANAGEMENT

FORECASTING FOR MANAGEMENT

WILLIAM K. BENTON
Zellerbach Paper Company
San Francisco, California

ADDISON-WESLEY PUBLISHING COMPANY
Reading, Massachusetts · Menlo Park, California · London · Don Mills, Ontario

This book is dedicated to all those who have been discouraged rather than enlightened by conventional mathematics and statistics texts, and to Stephen S. Waldron and Lan Li, who were patient.

PREFACE

This book is intended to introduce executives, planners, computer system analysts, and students to forecasting methods which are useful in management. Because the emphasis throughout is on *useful* techniques, rather than mathematically complex ones, the book differs in several ways from traditional forecasting texts.

For example, there is little discussion of applying differential calculus to curve fitting. While this and other classical techniques are interesting, the impact of the computer in recent years has made them virtually obsolete in the real world. Understanding what is happening, for instance, in the inventory control systems provided by IBM and other computer manufacturers is much more important. The topics presented here are those which have proven most useful in conjunction with computer methods, and the emphasis is on understanding the computer method and its relationship to the traditional approach.

Indeed, some of the methods introduced here are effective only because of the existence of high-speed computers. Simulation models and heuristic forecasting depend on an understanding of the forces at work, rather than on complex mathematical or statistical techniques; because they involve large masses of data, they only recently have become available for practical use. Modeling, in particular, is extremely valuable because it can be widely applied to business and planning problems—and it is far less technical than older methods.

This book is intended for nonmathematicians, and no mathematics or special skills beyond high school algebra are required, although a knowledge of FORTRAN or BASIC programming will enable the student to do certain exercises that could not otherwise be handled. But the book is written in English and is intended to be understood; while technical sections are included for reference, each is preceded by a nontechnical section (The Basic Idea) which explains the meaning and content in nontechnical language.

The ordinary reader, then, should simply read through the book, noting case examples related to his interests and skipping the technical parts. He

vii

can then return to the latter with at least some grasp of what's happening. It is important, however, to consider the questions and exercises which appear from time to time. These are not standard textbook-exercises; indeed, some of them have no solution. They are intended to raise important questions which will be dealt with in succeeding sections of the text.

I have relied heavily on case examples from my own consulting experience, that of my former colleagues at Arthur D. Little, Inc., and the technical literature. These actual cases help assure a practical viewpoint and point out, often dramatically, where forecasting methods have paid off most. These are the areas where government and private managers and planners—and students of business administration who will become managers and planners—need an understanding of the values, pitfalls, and basic concepts of computerized techniques. Specialists in many computer-related fields—statisticians, operations researchers, management scientists, systems analysts, and programmers—can provide technical expertise where it is called for—and often where it is not. This book is intended to provide the nonspecialist with a means of fighting back, as well as to provide students and forecasting system designers with a clear understanding of the new methods available to them.

San Francisco   W.K.B.
February 1972

CONTENTS

PART 1 | THE BASIC IDEA

CHAPTER 1

FUNDAMENTAL CONCEPTS

THE NEED FOR FORECASTING

In almost any activity, perfect knowledge of the future would be an immense advantage. In almost no activity, however, is certain knowledge available (except regarding death and taxes). Instead of certainty, we have uncertainty; no matter what we may expect tomorrow to bring, we know and admit that there is a chance something different will happen. Sometimes we are fairly certain that what we expect will occur; at other times we are very uncertain, and expect great changes.

In other words, our estimates of future events are subject to uncertainty. Less uncertainty is better than more, of course; zero uncertainty would be best, but it is not attainable. All the forecasting techniques discussed in this book have in common the basic goal of reducing the uncertainty in one's expectation of the future.

For example, here are some situations in which the value of reducing uncertainty is clear:

Stock prices. Obviously, knowing tomorrow's stock prices today could be a great advantage. Intuitively, without any special procedures or legerdemain, one knows that the price of a stock tomorrow is likely to be close to its price today, say within 20% above or below. However, that is the rub. One does not know whether it will be *above* or *below* today's price.

Of course, perfect knowledge isn't needed. Simply having a slightly better forecast than the others would give a stock market trader an advantage. There are two distinct schools of thought on predicting stock market prices. One claims that the price of a stock is a "random walk," which cannot be predicted on more than a statistical, average basis. Another school believes that there are ways of producing improved predictions, and is trying very hard to find them.

Duck hunting. A duck hunter sitting in a blind as ducks pass over engages in a good deal of forecasting activity. When he shoots at a duck, he must "lead" the bird by an amount which varies with the duck's height and speed. The

1

pellets from the shotgun will not reach the height at which the duck is flying until a second or two after the hunter pulls the trigger. The hunter, therefore, must *forecast* where the duck will be after a second or two, then attempt to place shot in the forecast spot at the requisite time.

The experience of generations of duck hunters has confirmed that there are no perfect forecasts. Therefore, instead of using a rifle, the hunter uses a shotgun which projects pellets into a *region*, which he hopes will cover the actual position of a duck in flight often enough to make the sport worthwhile. From the forecaster's point of view, this use of "spread" in shotgun loads is very significant. It reflects the fact that perfect forecasts are rare, that some uncertainty must be not only recognized but *provided for*, and that simply making appropriate provision for uncertainty can be very useful. It is also interesting to note that different amounts of spread are available in different makes of shotgun shells; in fact, some dedicated hunters prefer to pack their own so as to control the spread more accurately. A wider spread gives the hunter a better chance of hitting his mark, but at the expense of delivering less energy per unit area.

Antiaircraft fire. Not much statistical work has been done on the forecasting problem in duck hunting. However, an almost analogous problem has been intensively analyzed by some of the best technical brains available. This is the problem of forecasting the location of an aircraft. A defender trying to shoot down an attacking aircraft is faced with very much the same problem as the duck hunter, and very sophisticated forecasting routines have been developed to forecast aircraft positions. These have been built into the aiming mechanisms of antiaircraft guns. Some of them depend on ideas as simple as the "leading pattern" idea that the duck hunter uses, while others employ statistical notions having to do with the likelihood that the pilot will veer from his present course, which may in turn depend on the length of time he has flown in a straight line. (Question: Does the likelihood increase or decrease as the pilot continues to fly straight?)

The set of assumptions which the forecaster uses to predict a central value is called the *model*. The duck hunter's model is usually a steady trend, which extrapolates the duck's speed and direction; a sophisticated hunter might use a more complicated model involving wind velocity and even temperature and humidity. An airplane's expected position may be calculated in much the same way, or with additional variables which produce increased complexity.

The expected value of a stock may be calculated in a much more complicated way, often known only to the speculator. Only rarely is something as simple as extrapolation of past movements used. Many other examples could be discussed, but most of the important ones are closely analogous to stock markets, flights of ducks, or airplane paths. For reasons of practical importance, much effort has been spent in developing improved forecasting methods for:

Future demands for goods and services, so that appropriate inventory can be acquired and held to serve the demands. Sales forecasting in particular has stimulated as much wizardry as it has mathematics.

Sizes of markets, so that investments will be neither too large nor too small, and will hopefully produce neither overcapacity (and associated wasted investment), nor undercapacity (and associated lost sales).

Sizes of populations, such as the number of students expected to attend a given school in a given year. In a sense. this is an inventory problem, because the number of students corresponds to demand, and an inventory of teachers and books and the like must be acquired to service it; in another sense, it also corresponds to a market size, because the school can be thought of as an organization which vends education to a market consisting of students.

Prices and profits, for obvious reasons.

THE BASIC IDEA: MODELS AND ERRORS

In all the examples just discussed, and in nearly all the significant ones which arise in real life, the actual values of the thing to be forecast seem to cluster around a central point. The duck will usually be close to, say, 20 feet ahead of his initial position when the shot reaches his altitude. The airplane likewise will be about so many yards or miles ahead of its present position. The price of a stock tomorrow will in general be close to its price today; if you look only at stocks whose prices are declining, for instance, you might guess that the central point will be a few percent lower. From a more complex point of view, the point about which the prices of a given stock may cluster tomorrow is today's price discounted by a percentage reflecting recent changes in that stock. Or you might base your discount on changes in the market as a whole, indicated by a market average like the Dow Jones Industrials Average. (Question: Is it easier to predict tomorrow's value of a market indicator or of an individual stock? Keep in mind that the indicator's value is simply an average of the value of the stocks. Is the recent history of an individual stock a better guide to its immediate future than the recent history of the market as a whole?)

As these examples show, the forecasting problem can be broken into two parts. One part of the problem is to predict the value of the central point among possible future values; the other has to do with measuring the expected scatter of actual events around this forecast midpoint. Thus the duck hunter may aim at a point 20 feet ahead of the duck and deal with the error by the scatter of the pellets; the stock market trader may predict a price 10% above or 10% below today's prices, and protect himself against the uncertainty of his forecast by selling short or by holding some cash in reserve. In both cases, the forecaster acts as though there were a single expected value and an associated range of possible errors.

Graphs as Models
It is often convenient to portray the model of a variable we are interested in predicting as a graph, showing the expected or central value of the variable as it changes with time, or sometimes as it relates to some other independent variable. The use of graphs removes the need for complicated mathematical formulas describing the curve; formulas can be supplied later when more accuracy is desired. For example:

1. A duck is flying north of a hunter at a steady rate in a straight line. The hunter wants to predict the duck's position when the shot reaches it, assuming that the hunter fires when the duck is directly overhead. A simple graph, shown in Fig. 1–1, indicates the predicted position of the duck at different heights from the ground, using its position when the hunter fires as zero-point.

2. Sales of an item have been increasing 10% a year. The simple graph in Fig. 1–2 indicates a model for forecasting this item's sales in future years.

3. Figure 1–3 is a rough graph indicating a model which could be used for forecasting sales of a new type of antifreeze just coming into general use in New England. A second line shows expected sales of the older, less effective antifreeze which is being replaced. Because of seasonal variation, this model is not a smooth curve like the earlier examples, but it is just as simple. The model is based on an inverse relationship; during the significant selling periods, sales of the old product decline roughly in proportion to increased sales of the new type.

Whether he converts it into a mathematical formula or not, a forecaster always employs a model of the process he is interested in when making a forecast. And whether or not he recognizes the uncertainty in his forecast— so that he calls it a "guess" rather than a forecast—the forecaster is almost never surprised to find that his observation of what actually transpires is a bit different from what he forecast earlier. The forecaster's model usually attempts to reflect each force which he believes affects the process at work, but he can never include in his model *all* of the forces which affect the process; in fact, he usually deliberately leaves out a number of factors which he acknowledges to exist. For instance, the duck hunter may not even try to take account of the possibility of a sudden gust of wind; the antiaircraft gunner does not try to take account of changes in the weight of fuel carried; the stock market forecaster may not be aware of an extra dividend payment or new product which will affect the price of his stock. Whether or not the forecaster is aware of them, such factors may affect his results.

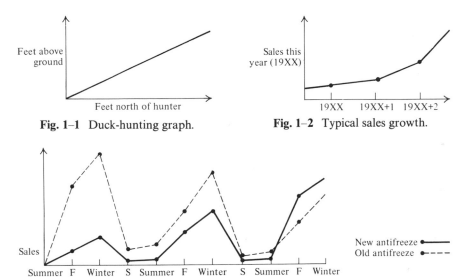

Fig. 1–1 Duck-hunting graph.   **Fig. 1–2** Typical sales growth.

Fig. 1–3 Cyclical sales growth with inverse relationship.

The more factors included in a model, the more likely the model is to be accurate *if* the factors added to the model, and their actual effects, are clearly understood. "More accurate," of course, means that the forecast errors are smaller. On the one hand, additional understanding of the forces at work in a process can improve forecasting by producing a more sophisticated model; on the other hand, adding factors whose influence is only guessed at and not known for certain is almost sure to reduce the accuracy of a forecast. This is partly because people naturally tend to overemphasize small but newly recognized factors, and partly for statistical reasons which will be discussed later. The net result is that simple models are usually much more accurate than complex ones. It is hard to keep this in mind when thinking about your business, but it is true.

A convenient way to summarize the influence of known and unknown factors is to say that the actual forecast results correspond to two sets of factors. One set, known as *assignable* causes, consists of processes which are understood, whose influence can be evaluated, and which can be built into a model. There is always a difference between the forecast produced by a model based on these assignable causes and the actual course of events; the difference is called forecast error, and it is convenient to think of it as the result of the other set of causes, the *nonassignable* values. For this reason, forecasting models are nearly always described in two parts:

$$\text{Forecast} = \text{Model} + \text{Error}.$$

The forecaster naturally tries to make the error portion of his forecast as small as possible, but this can involve him in the complexity we just warned against, or can cost too much in time and money even if it does produce improved results. Actually, he can make the error factor work for him, and we will return to this topic at length in a later section.

TYPES OF FORECASTING

Three main methods of dealing with the future are useful in corporate, government, and other organizational planning. These three general types of forecasting activities correspond to the three central sections of this book. They are structural forecasting, time-series forecasting, and forecasting methods based on the notion of using errors.

Structural Forecasting

The most direct form of forecasting is modeling, in which an explicit description of the forces at work and their effects is used to provide a step-by-step picture of a probable sequence of events. A good example of the type of factor used in simulation can be drawn from sales forecasting: One can model the marketing operation by assuming a relationship between the number of salesmen employed and the number of sales they produce. For instance, in predicting sales for a life insurance company, it could be assumed that each salesman will sell 10 policies per month. This assumption, together with information on the number of salesmen actually employed, can be used to forecast the number of policies which will be sold in successive months. A variety of other information—such as the average value of each policy, the probability that an existing policy will be canceled, and information about different types of markets or different policies—can then be used to build a detailed model and produce a working forecast.

A very detailed attempt to picture an economic process is called a *simulation* model; a simplified version which is acknowledged to be incomplete but is still of interest is called an *heuristic* model. No statistical methods need to be involved in simple models of these types. On the other hand, models usually involve a great deal of arithmetic and tabulation. As a result, models generally need to be programmed for a computer if they are to be useful.

Despite their apparent simplicity of use, however, these structural models can be one of the trickiest forecasting methods to use. The fact that there are no ready-made equations involved means that you must make up your own, and that in turn means that you must understand the structure of the process you are studying and the effects of all the factors which enter into it. The research and thought necessary to arrive at such understanding are usually very valuable in themselves, and are often rewarded with a more accurate forecast than can be obtained by any other means; but if they are not done thoroughly it is better not to attempt this method at all.

Time-Series Forecasting

Sequences of numbers which can be extrapolated into the future are called *time series*. These numbers may be sales figures, population figures, profits, losses, or almost anything else. Typically, though not always, the list of such numbers is generated by producing one value for successive time periods (such as the sales of a given product in each month). This accounts for the name "time series." As a matter of interest, statisticians have been analyzing time series and searching for better ways to forecast future values for many years; the longest series known—that of spring flood heights of the Nile River*—was begun over 4000 years ago. Time series which arise in business tend to have a structure composed of random variation around some central pattern. The trick lies in guessing what the central pattern is and measuring the variation.

The Uses of Uncertainty

In time series or any other type of forecasting, no one expects the forecast to be exactly correct. There is always some error; the expected error reflects

---

* For examples, see Emil J. Gumbel, *Statistics of Extremes*, Columbia University Press, New York, 1958.

uncertainty about the future. There are many ways in which this lack of perfection can be dealt with so as to minimize its effects, and there are also some ways, mostly statistical, which can be used to capitalize on the uncertainty. This subject is discussed in detail in Part 4 of this book.

Using Forecasting Systems

The way you use a forecasting method, any method, is even more important than the method itself. Using a carefully chosen method may reduce forecasting error by 20% or 50%; presenting the results incomprehensibly or misleadingly may make the results 100% or 1000% wrong. Therefore, the final major section of this book is devoted to ways of making effective the methods previously explained.

Clear explanations and tact have always been necessary in presenting statistical results to management. Today, the computer can immensely compound the confusion and resentment that may occur. Forecasts, for instance, are often presented to nontechnical people as "computer forecasts" rather than "statistical forecasts." This view leads to several types of problems in organizing the forecasting activity within a business or governmental organization. The problems that arise and the available solutions are slightly different in the development of a forecasting system from those encountered in the routine use of one; public and private organizations have somewhat different needs, and, of course, large organizations and small organizations usually need to be handled differently.

The problems and management techniques discussed in the final section of the book are, of course, applicable to many areas besides that of forecasting systems, but the roles of computers and statistics in forecasting are outstanding examples of the problems of technical knowledge in management. While this section is short and nontechnical, it is certainly as important as the rest, both to the forecasting technician and to the manager who needs to deal with technicians.

READING, WRITING, AND COMPUTERS

As you get used to the concepts of forecasting and the way in which they are discussed, a number of terms will become familiar. The first of these is the abbreviation of "the value forecast by using the model" to "the model," which simplifies some rather cumbrous phrases. It is much simpler to say, "The model was 24 but the actual was $25\frac{1}{2}$," than to say, "While the value predicted by the model was 24 the value actually observed in the event was $25\frac{1}{2}$." The summary equation used earlier, "Forecast = Model + Error," is, of course, a contraction of a sentence which uses the phrase "the value of the" a number of times, confusingly.

Words are often shortened to their initials, so that "forecast" becomes F. Model does not become M, however; it becomes P (for "prediction") or XHAT, from the statistician's symbol for the forecast value of a variable, which is $\hat{X}$. Error is usually represented by the small Greek epsilon (ε); in this book we will use the more familiar Roman E, so that the summary becomes:

$$F = P + E.$$

In view of the central role played by computers in forecasting for business and government today, statements in this book are generally shown the way they are written for computers. The result should familiarize the reader with computer-oriented phrasing, and make it easier for him to read and interpret actual computer documents. For instance, capital letters are used because computer printouts and computer programs contain only capital letters. Also, subscripts are avoided. Where a mathematician or statistician in a university might write a_t, we would write A(T). Finally, the asterisk ($*$) is used for multiplication, to avoid confusion with the letter X. Division is indicated by the slash, as in A/B and 2/3.

The computer language most widely used in statistical applications such as forecasting is called FORTRAN. The name comes from the phrase *FORmula TRANslator*. It was the first in a series of successful attempts by computer people to produce ways of communicating with the computer which are similar to ordinary English, but still unambiguous and clear enough for computer use. Before such computer languages were developed, computers had to be given instructions as long lists of numbers. The numbers corresponded to specific commands such as add and subtract, or read and write, and translating the commands from English into the numerical codes demanded great effort on the part of the programmers. Since the computer is made for just such dull and demanding work, the job has now been handed over to it: A computer language is really a computer program, designed to translate English or near-English into the numerical codes required inside the computer.

PART 2 | STRUCTURAL FORECASTING

CHAPTER 2

MODELING AND SIMULATION

The essence of *every* forecasting method is the model which is used to describe the underlying process. Many standard types of model exist, from the very simple trend line through more complex types like relational models, to the sophisticated Markov chain. But because these are standard methods, the word model is only a part of their names, and we tend to think of them as abstract techniques rather than as pictures of actual processes. It is when we come up against a situation which cannot adequately be described by one of the standard methods that we become aware again of the original meaning of the term.

THE BASIC IDEA

The process of inventing a new model to describe a situation which is not conveniently mirrored by one of the standard types is called *modeling*. If the model is sufficiently detailed, the process is called *simulation*. Such models are unique, by definition, but the process of constructing them can be deduced from studying a few examples.

The examples discussed below have been specifically chosen for their significance to executive planning. The first is a forecasting model for a proposed business venture; the second is a model of residential real estate in an entire city; the third is another forecasting model for land use in the same area, which uses a different technique.

FORECASTING A NEW VENTURE BY SIMULATION

A group of young men with experience in hospital administration and in data processing conceived the idea of offering a data processing service to hospitals. The unique aspect of their service was to be the type of communications they offered to their clients. They planned to put a small computer terminal in each hospital, and to use that terminal to enter data directly into the computer from the hospital business offices. The terminal would also print out patients' bills on request, eliminating the problem of long delays in getting the data from the hospital to the computer center and in getting bills out to patients. The entrepreneurs thought this would give them a competitive advantage.

On the other hand, this approach had an effect on the cost of their operation. They would have to provide a terminal, at a cost of about $300 per month, for each customer who signed up. So the expenditure on equipment would be equal to the cost of the central computer, about $10,000 per month, plus $300 times the number of customers.

The number of customers, of course, would start out at zero, but as salesmen were hired and began selling, the number should increase. On the basis of their experience in the field, the entrepreneurs estimated that a good salesman might land one new account every three months, on the average. Each customer who signed up could be expected to produce revenue, but could also be expected to produce several new costs.

The computer terminal would be one of those costs; another would be the personnel required to assist the customer in beginning to use the new system. Conversion to a new system of data processing involves a large amount of set-up work, whether the previous system was computerized or manual. If computerized, records will usually have to be translated into new forms or formats; if manual, data will probably have to be gathered from widely scattered sources before the translation process can begin. New forms must be designed for gathering the data and for printing the output—in this case, the patient's bill. And myriad practical details must be worked out: time schedules for entering data and receiving completed work, new personnel responsibilities and operational procedures, and the like. For instance, having a terminal in the hospital would mean that a terminal operator must be hired—if no suitable person exists in the present operation—and trained to run the machine. Conversion usually requires the assistance of one or more conversion specialists from the data processing service. The conversion of a typical hospital, the entrepreneurs estimated, would require two conversion specialists for a period of six months.

These examples suggest an overall structure for forecasting the net income of the proposed service center. All of the relationships among sales, income, and cost should be defined explicitly. The dollar figures which measure each of those costs, such as salaries for salesmen and conversion specialists, rental of equipment, and the like, should then be fitted into the formulas. Then the entire system should be converted into a computer program, which could do the following for each month:

1. Compute the number of sales expected, on the basis of the number of salesmen who have been hired.

2. Calculate from this the total number of customers, new and old.

3. Calculate variable personnel costs related to the total numbers of customers and to new customers. For instance, account executives and service representatives must be continually available to all customers; conversion specialists need be available for new customers only.

4. Calculate the revenue corresponding to the total number of customers.

5. Include such fixed costs as the rent for the center, general overhead, salary of the manager, etc.

6. Compute net income for the month.

7. Compute net income to date.

Using a Venture Simulation Model

A computer program which accomplishes the steps listed above is really a simulation of the new venture, or at least of its financial aspects. Once the program is written, it can be used to evaluate the attractiveness of the new idea, assuming, of course, that the relationships have been described correctly and that the cost and income figures are reasonable. In this particular case, the model showed clearly that there were several distinct phases of operation, each with a different financial picture. Phase 1, which we have not previously mentioned, would require large investment in developing the system: writing, testing, and debugging necessary programs, preparing user manuals and other documentation, perhaps doing research on alternative types of terminals and central computers, and so on. This phase might continue for a year.

At the end of this development period, salesmen are hired, trained, and sent into the field. They begin generating actual customers in Phase 2. This active selling phase continues until the capacity of the center is reached. That is, it continues until no new accounts can be accepted without major changes. At that point, assuming that only one center is contemplated, the sales force will be reduced or eliminated, and the profit figures should reflect these savings.

This sequence of events means that a large investment in Phase 1 must be made up by profits in Phases 2 and 3. To find out if that will indeed take place, the computer forecasting simulation can be run for several simulated years, beginning at the start of Phase 1.

The result is a sequence of monthly income figures and net-income-to-date figures. These figures are the bottom lines in Figs. 2–2 through 2–4; Fig. 2–1 is a list of the assumptions made by the model. They were printed at the beginning of the computer run for convenient reference.

```
CASH FLOW ANALYSIS FOR DATA PROCESSING CENTER


CONSTANT PERSONNEL ASSUMPTIONS FOR THIS RUN
   0 SYSTEM ANALYSIS AT $16000
   0 PROGRAMMERS AT $14000
   1 CENTER MANAGER AT $16000
   5 OPERATORS,CLERKS,ETC. AT $8000



REVENUE ASSUMPTIONS ARE

EACH SALESMAN MAKES ONE SALE EVERY THREE MONTHS

WITH 200 BEDS, $1.00/PATIENT DAY, AND 80 PCT OCC, REV =   $   4500.00

CENTRAL COMPUTER RENTAL                                      10000.00

GENERAL OVERHEAD $                                            5000.00

RENTAL OF EACH TERMINAL   $                                    300.00

VARIABLE PERSONNEL COSTS

  SALESMANS SALARY INCLUDING COMMISSION                      18000.00

  CUSTOMER REPRESENTATIVES SALARY   $                        15000.00

  CUSTOMER EXECUTIVES SALARY INCLUDING EXPENSES  $           25000.00

THERE IS ONE CUSTOMER REPRESENTATIVE FOR EVERY 3 CUSTOMERS

THERE IS ONE CUSTOMER EXECUTIVE FOR EVERY 5 CUSTOMERS

EACH CUSTOMER REQUIRES TWO CONVERSION SPECIALISTS FOR 6 MO

TAXES ARE ALWAYS ZERO
```

Fig. 2–1 Assumptions for a simulation model run.

The numbers which are calculated in a run of the computer model are used first by inspection. The entrepreneurs and their financial resource analysts reviewed these results to determine whether the investment was worthwhile. In this case the results were encouraging. But the model would have been equally useful if the results had been otherwise: In that case, it would have saved the partners from a costly and unprofitable investment.

Testing Alternative Strategies

The ease with which we can change some of the assumptions of a forecasting simulation model and run it again leads to the second way of using it. Suppose customer accounts produced a different average revenue; how would that affect the venture? Or suppose sales were slower, and a salesman sold new accounts at an average of one every six months, instead of one every

YEAR 1

NBR CUSTOMER	7	6	5	5	4	4	3	3	2	1	1	0
REVENUE	13500	13500	9000	4500	4500	0	0	0	0	0	0	0
SALESMEN	3000	3000	3000	3000	3000	3000	3000	3000	3000	3000	3000	3000
CONVERSION E	0	0	0	0	0	0	0	0	0	0	0	0
CUST REPRS	2500	1250	1250	1250	1250	1250	0	0	0	0	0	0
CUST EXECS	2083	2083	2083	2083	0	0	0	0	0	0	0	0
EQUIP COST	10000	10000	10000	10000	10000	10000	10000	10000	10000	10000	10000	10000
LINE COST	2100	1800	1500	1500	1200	1200	900	900	600	300	300	0
LOAN	0	0	0	0	0	0	0	0	0	0	0	0
SYSTEM ANALY	0	0	0	0	0	0	0	0	0	0	0	0
PROGRAMMERS	0	0	0	0	0	0	0	0	0	0	0	0
OPERATORS	3333	3333	3333	3333	3333	3333	3333	3333	3333	3333	3333	3333
MANAGER	1333	1333	1333	1333	1333	1333	1333	1333	1333	1333	1333	1333
OVERHEAD	5000	5000	5000	5000	5000	5000	5000	5000	5000	5000	5000	5000
	0	0	0	0	0	0	0	0	0	0	0	0
	0	0	0	0	0	0	0	0	0	0	0	0
	0	0	0	0	0	0	0	0	0	0	0	0
TOTALS	0	0	0	0	0	0	0	0	0	0	0	0
EXPENSES	29350	27800	27500	27500	25117	25117	23567	23567	23267	22967	22967	22667
NET INCOME	-15850	-14300	-18500	-23000	-20617	-25117	-23567	-23567	-23267	-22967	-22967	-22667
CUMULATIVE	-256383	-240533	-226233	-207733	-184733	-164117	-139000	-115433	-91867	-68600	-45633	-22667

Fig. 2-2 Results for Year 1 of operation.

YEAR 2

NBR CUSTOMER	7	8	8	9	10	10	11	11	12	13	13	14
REVENUE	18000	18000	22500	22500	27000	31500	31500	36000	36000	40500	45000	45000
SALESMEN	3000	3000	3000	3000	3000	3000	3000	3000	3000	3000	3000	3000
CONVERSION E	0	0	0	0	0	0	0	0	0	0	0	0
CUST REPRS	2500	2500	2500	2500	3750	3750	3750	3750	3750	5000	5000	5000
CUST EXECS	2083	2083	2083	2083	4167	4167	4167	4167	4167	4167	4167	4167
EQUIP COST	10000	10000	10000	10000	10000	10000	10000	10000	10000	10000	10000	10000
LINE COST	2100	2400	2400	2700	3000	3000	3300	3300	3600	3900	3900	4200
LOAN	0	0	0	0	0	0	0	0	0	0	0	0
SYSTEM ANALY	0	0	0	0	0	0	0	0	0	0	0	0
PROGRAMMERS	0	0	0	0	0	0	0	0	0	0	0	0
OPERATORS	3333	3333	3333	3333	3333	3333	3333	3333	3333	3333	3333	3333
MANAGER	1333	1333	1333	1333	1333	1333	1333	1333	1333	1333	1333	1333
OVERHEAD	5000	5000	5000	5000	5000	5000	5000	5000	5000	5000	5000	5000
	0	0	0	0	0	0	0	0	0	0	0	0
	0	0	0	0	0	0	0	0	0	0	0	0
TOTALS	0	0	0	0	0	0	0	0	0	0	0	0
EXPENSES	29350	29650	29650	29950	33583	33583	33883	33883	34183	35733	35733	36033
NET INCOME	-11350	-11650	-7150	-7450	-6583	-2083	-2383	2117	1817	4767	9267	8967
CUMULATIVE	-267733	-279383	-286533	-296963	-300567	-302650	-305033	-302917	-301100	-296333	-267067	-276100

Fig. 2–3 Results for Year 2 of operation.

YEAR 3

NBR CUSTOMER	14	14	14	14	14	14	14	14	14	14	14
REVENUE	49500	54000	58500	58500	63000	63000	63000	63000	63000	63000	63000
SALESMEN	0	0	0	0	0	0	0	0	0	0	0
CONVERSION E	0	0	0	0	0	0	0	0	0	0	0
CUST REPRS	5000	5000	5000	5000	5000	5000	5000	5000	5000	5000	5000
CUST EXECS	4167	4167	4167	4167	4167	4167	4167	4167	4167	4167	4167
EQUIP COST	10000	10000	10000	10000	10000	10000	10000	10000	10000	10000	10000
LINE COST	4200	4200	4200	4200	4200	4200	4200	4200	4200	4200	4200
LOAN	0	0	0	0	0	0	0	0	0	0	0
SYSTEM ANALY	0	0	0	0	0	0	0	0	0	0	0
PROGRAMMERS	0	0	0	0	0	0	0	0	0	0	0
OPERATORS	3333	3333	3333	3333	3333	3333	3333	3333	3333	3333	3333
MANAGER	1333	1333	1333	1333	1333	1333	1333	1333	1333	1333	1333
OVERHEAD	5000	5000	5000	5000	5000	5000	5000	5000	5000	5000	5000
	0	0	0	0	0	0	0	0	0	0	0
	0	0	0	0	0	0	0	0	0	0	0
TOTALS	0	0	0	0	0	0	0	0	0	0	0
EXPENSES	33033	33033	33033	33033	33033	33033	33033	33033	33033	33033	33033
NET INCOME	16467	20967	25467	25467	29967	29967	29967	29967	29967	29967	29967
CUMULATIVE	-261633	-245167	-224200	-198733	-173267	-143300	-113333	-83367	-53400	-23433	6533	36500

Fig. 2–4 Results for Year 3 of operation.

three months? Testing changes like these requires only the changing of a few punched cards and the rerunning of the computer program. The additional cost is only a few dollars, and the time required is less than a day.

In short, once a forecasting procedure or simulation of this type is developed, it can be used to forecast income and profit under different sets of assumptions. For instance, in an operation like this hospital service center, the time at which salesmen are hired and the number hired are crucial factors. Both expenses and sales rise in proportion to the number of salesmen; when many salesmen are hired, sales should be higher than otherwise, but expenses will also be higher. And if too many are hired at once, expenses may in fact be so high that they cannot be covered by any reasonable source of capital. This sort of problem is a common one in new ventures. To investigate the effects of hiring two, three, four, or more salesmen, a separate run of the forecasting simulation can be made with each different number.

A simulation can thus guide the user to the best strategy, simply by enabling him to forecast the effects of the different strategies from which he may choose. The overall result of this use is not only to tell the user what return he can expect for a given strategy, but also to tell him which is the best return he can get. Therefore, simulations like this are a very useful and practical kind of forecasting tool.

Another Example of New Venture Simulation

Many analyses of this kind have been done. A very similar one, done to forecast income from a proposed timesharing service, was reported in DATAMATION magazine.* The general outline of the forecasting model is similar, but a number of slight differences appears. Most of them reflect differences between the hospital accounting business and the timesharing field, and this underscores the primary importance of understanding the processes at work.

For instance, the timesharing business is characterized both by growth in revenue from a given account as time passes, and by a fair chance that a given account will switch to a competitor. Accounts in timesharing tend to be much smaller on the average than hospital accounting customers. So the model which was built includes an increasing income from each customer where the hospital account model assumes a steady rate, and it includes explicit calculations of losses due to customers switching away.

---

* Yourdon, Edward, "Call/360 Costs," *DATAMATION*, Nov. 1970, pp. 22–28.

FORECASTING SIMULATION OF AN ENTIRE CITY

Forecasting models can be far more elaborate than the new business example. For instance, the San Francisco City Planning Department participated in the development of a simulation model to be used for forecasting future changes in the residential portions of the city. This was part of a large-scale attempt to forecast the overall development of San Francisco. Just as in the new venture analysis, the relationships among various factors and the changes they produced were analyzed and written down explicitly. These relationships were then converted into a computer program. Vast quantities of numerical data were obtained and entered: the rents on various types of space, the numbers of each type of building, and numerous other facts had to be defined, analyzed, collected, and processed.

Focus on Reasons

The central focus in modeling, as in any forecasting simulation, must be on understanding the forces which lead to change. In the case of the new venture, change was assumed to be the result of sales activity, and the change consisted of adding new customers and the associated income and expenditure. In the case of changes in a city's residential housing, the forces at work are mainly economic. The situation can be visualized as the classic supply–demand problem, in which a strong demand for a type of housing in short supply will produce an increase in the price and therefore profitability of that type. According to economic theory, this should prompt investors to build more of that type of housing. If one knew enough facts about the demand of different types of people for various housing types, and had accurate information about the available supplies of those types, one should be able to identify those for which the demand outstrips the supply. A computer model should be able to do the actual work of comparing demand and supply for each type of housing.

But simple desire alone is not enough to guarantee that a given building type will actually be profitable if an investor builds it. Although we all might like to have a 40-room mansion with two swimming pools, the effective demand for such buildings is not very great. On the other hand, while inability to pay reduces the effective demand for a given type of housing, unavailability of certain preferred types will increase the effective demand for other types. For instance, if there are too few single-family dwellings, there may be an overflow of families with children into the next preferred type of housing, possibly two-bedroom garden apartments.

Moreover, in a city like San Francisco, nearly all available land is already built upon. Building new residential housing therefore is not a simple matter of filling up open space. Instead, it corresponds to replacing an existing, relatively low-profit type of building with a new, higher-profit type of building. The low-profit building should be identifiable on the basis of low demand, just as potentially high-profit types can be. Once again, the computer should be able to do the actual work.

The computer would have to be told how many units of each type of housing are available at the beginning of the forecasting run, and then keep track of effective demand for—and supply of—each type. The available supply will be reduced by spillover of demand for unavailable types, and the computer will have to keep track of this, too. It will also have to add and subtract units in the supply as buildings are erected and demolished in the simulation. Although each step is simple, in all there is quite a high level of complexity, and quite a lot of simple arithmetic. The advantage of doing it by computer rather than by hand should be obvious.

Working Out the Model

The overall pattern of interacting forces which affect the city's residential housing was worked out in detail by a team of economists, system analysts, and computer specialists. In contrast to the new venture example discussed earlier, at the beginning of the San Francisco project the participants had no idea what their model might be like. The data processing partners understood the needs of hospitals well enough to be able to outline what would happen when they put salesmen in the field, but the working of a city is so complex that a great deal of research was needed before even a simple list of steps could be constructed for the housing process.

For example, builders require a minimum level of profitability before they will invest in a new venture. This meant that the model had to calculate the cost and return of each possible new venture, calculate its probable profitability, and then decide whether that profitability was high enough for a builder to want to invest. But the required level of profitability is different for different types of builders. An apartment complex developer will typically require a higher return on his investment than a small builder of single-family homes. Simply finding out what profitability level each different kind of builder required before he would make an investment was in itself a major research project carried out by a small team of researchers.

This was only one of a variety of studies which had to be done in order to fill in the general outlines of the model suggested above. Defining "types" of housing, "residential areas," measures of desirability, and other factors each required comparable effort. The research which went into simply understanding the processes well enough to model them cost several hundred thousand dollars. The modeling itself, translating each of those definitions into numerical terms and equations with which the computer could work, again required a large investment. The level of effort here is obviously far greater than that involved in the new venture analysis described above, which in fact took only about one man-week of work.

The general outlines of the San Francisco model are shown in Fig. 2–5. Figure 2–6 shows sections from the beginning of the detailed flow chart. The complexity of this model is significant because it represents a minimum level of detail for simulation of any but the simplest social and economic processes.

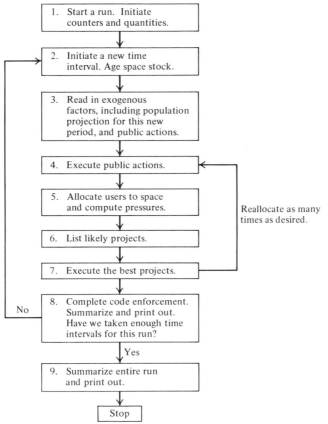

Fig. 2–5 Simplified flow chart. Source: Model of San Francisco Housing Market, Arthur D. Little, Inc., Cambridge, Mass., Jan. 1966.

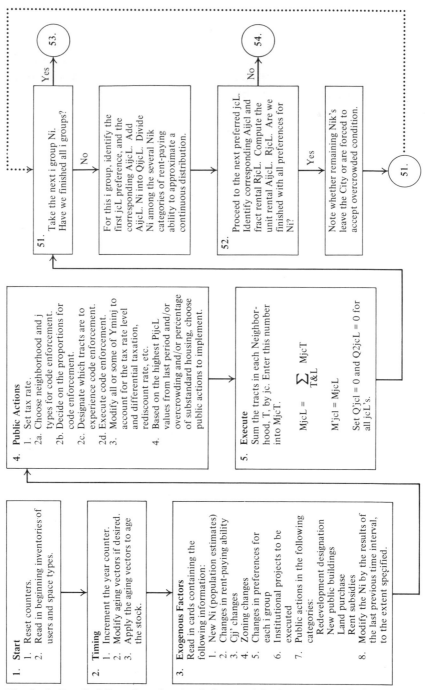

Fig. 2–6 Detailed flow chart for simulation model. Source: Model of San Francisco Housing Market, Arthur D. Little, Inc., Cambridge, Mass., Jan. 1966.

Use of the Model

The model was intended to help the city planning staff forecast changes in the city. To use the model, the staff could specify any set of public actions they were interested in evaluating, convert these into computer input form, and then run the computer model.

The city might, for example, change height limits for apartment buildings, make zoning changes, designate areas as redevelopment districts, or build public low-income housing. The model could be run to indicate the effects of each of these actions. Low-cost public housing, for instance, would affect the number of low- and middle-income units built by private developers, and might ultimately change the city's tax base.

The model "demolished" and "built" new buildings, in accordance with the concept outlined above, for nine simulated years. The computer printed out the actions taken and a variety of summary information, such as the forecast number of buildings of each type at the end of each two-year period.

How Well Did it Work?

The research, design, and computer programming aspects of the San Francisco simulation model were highly successful. This is not always the case; many models of equivalent complexity have never run at all. The San Francisco model not only ran, but also produced reasonable forecasts in the several runs carried out by the City Planning Department.

Several tests were made after the model was completed, in which the model was used to forecast construction activity in the past few years on the basis of input data for previous years, in combination with the public actions that had actually taken place. The results were overall quite accurate; the total number of housing units "built" by the model was within 1% of the total number actually built in the historical period. Within specific types of housing, such as small apartment houses, single-family houses, and large apartment houses, larger errors were observed; but this is not at all unusual for statistical forecasting models: Errors within categories cancel out to produce an accurate overall result.

Even if the model were less accurate, it would still be useful for evaluating the effects of alternate public actions. For instance, if the model were asked to suppose the addition of a large block of public low-cost housing, it would probably indicate some influence on the number of smaller apartment buildings created, changing their number either upward or downward. The *direction* of change would still be significant, or at least suggestive, even if the absolute numbers were suspected of some error.

But in fact, these comparison runs were never made and from the viewpoint of actual use the model was a dismal failure. Extensive studies have been made of the construction and use of this particular model; they are listed in the Bibliography. It appears that the reason for failure was psychological rather than technical. The city planners who were supposed to use the model seem to have been suspicious of the exaggerated claims for statistical modeling made by some of the technical team members, and were very cautious about accepting the computer methods involved. In short, they didn't believe in it. The model had been constructed under oppressive time and budget deadlines, and the crash nature of the effort probably left less than the necessary time available for public relations and communications. The lesson here will be considered again in the section on use of forecasting systems at the end of this book.

HEURISTIC FORECASTING

An heuristic is basically a simplified simulation. Both types of simulation attempt to reflect the workings of a process by specifying the actual effects of changes in independent variables. These independent variables are those that may be controlled; in the examples above the independent variables were the number of salesmen in a new venture and the number of public housing units constructed by a city planning agency.

The difference between a simulation model and an heuristic model lies in the degree of detail. The simulation model attempts to represent every facet of the operation accurately, and extensive tests of accuracy are included in development. In this way, simulation modeling is very much like scientific research. Heuristic models, on the other hand, make use of educated guesses, rules of thumb, and reasonable estimates. They are structurally similar to simulation models, but since they rely on judgment rather than on research into how a process works, they can be constructed much more quickly and easily.

The use of judgment and educated guesses in constructing a model has both beneficial and harmful effects. The main beneficial effect is in making the forecasting model comprehensible and sensible. And since heuristic models are usually simpler and more general than detailed simulations, they make the job of programming easier. On the other hand, the use of a rule of thumb or even an educated guess—any procedure which is not rigorously and scientifically validated before being used—can sometimes lead to real errors. More important, incorrect guesses and erroneous assumptions are not corrected but instead are built upon.

The San Francisco simulation described above was based on units consisting of individual structures or groups of structures occupying a couple of square blocks. A less detailed model for the San Francisco Bay Area as a whole has also been created. This heuristic project is the Bay Area Simulation Study (BASS), which does very much the same thing the San Francisco simulation does, but tries to do it in a considerably simpler way.

The BASS computer program is given forecasts of employment for 21 industries in all 13 counties of the Bay Area, and specific population forecasts for each county. It is also given information on the real-estate status of the counties at the beginning of the run, representing the present. This includes land inventory for various categories, housing units of different types in each subarea, and the distribution of population in each subarea. The computer run then produces:

1. employment forecasts for each industry in each area,

2. housing unit forecasts for each category in each subarea,

3. population forecasts for each subarea, and

4. land-use forecasts for each category in each subarea.

The outputs of the BASS program, then, are similar to the outputs of the San Francisco simulation. Both indicate the type of housing which can be expected to develop, in what quantity and in what location. The main difference is that the San Francisco simulation tries to simulate the builders' actual decision-making process, whereas the BASS computer model simply decides how much new housing is needed on the basis of population forecasts and allocates this new housing to the various subareas "as a function of the accessibility and holding capacity of each subarea." For instance, apartment buildings are assigned to subareas which are near good employment areas and have good transportation links to them, while single-family units are distributed in less expensive outlying areas.*

Both the San Francisco simulation and the BASS heuristic produce roughly the same kind of results. Both models' forecasts should be regarded as suggestive rather than as exact numerical expectations; the difference is in how they do it.

---

* For more details, see *Jobs, People, and Land,* by the Staff, the Center for Real Estate and Urban Economics, Institute of Urban and Regional Development (University of California, Berkeley, 1968), p. 22.

The Uses of Area Models

It should be obvious from the two examples described above that the use of simulation or heuristic models in forecasting real-estate use is still in the experimental stage. A great deal of money is required to produce results which may then be disbelieved, as in the case of the San Francisco model; or, as with the BASS model, the information may not be sufficiently precise to be used, for instance, as a basis for private investment.

On the other hand, it seems clear that even the heuristic results of the BASS model provide a coherent and rational summary of what is likely to happen. This sort of rationalization in viewing the future can be very useful, especially in working with as large a system as the 13-county Bay Area.

Public officials can make very effective use of such large-scale models as they attempt to decide what steps would be needed, beneficial, harmful, or disastrous in providing public sector support, and the results can provide important background for businessmen. A city or regional forecasting model might not be able to tell you whether to build on Post Street or on Sutter, but it could probably indicate whether it is worthwhile building at all. And with more and more areas currently investing in such analyses, it may become possible to compare widely scattered locations through complete demographic models. These might include population, wage, industry, and other trends as well as real-estate factors, any of which might be decisive in choosing, say, your next warehouse site.

SOME OTHER MODELS

Many other types of forecasting models have been developed for use in conjunction with computers. Most of them fall in between the simulation and heuristic models of this chapter, which try to depict a specific situation as accurately as possible, and the more general relationship models described in the next chapter. The models discussed briefly below are less often useful in practical situations than the other methods considered in this chapter, and they are included here largely for the sake of completeness. On the other hand, they have had some very useful applications and, perhaps more important, they provide additional conceptual models for forecasting. Both Markov chains and input-output models are based on especially coherent and intellectually appealing concepts. The input-output method in particular seems to be very useful for visualizing very large-scale economic phenomena such as national and international economies, and it has been applied to the internal operations of at least one large corporation. Even if you never actually use the concepts presented below as the basis of a forecasting procedure or a computer program, it doesn't hurt to be aware of them; there is a lot to be said for anything that enables us to think more clearly.

I-O Models

Some economic models attempt to reflect the basic influences in an economic region as a whole, so that growth and decline in that region can be forecast. The idea of business cycles has attracted much interest, but has produced no useful results so far. On the other hand, the input-output economic model has been quite useful. Input-output (I-O) models try to reflect the basic relationships between different sectors of the economy. For example, there is a very clear relationship between the construction industry and the plywood industry. There is a less obvious relationship, but an equally real one, between the plywood industry and the mill machinery industry, and also between the machinery business and the construction industry. These relationships are all buyer–seller relationships, and a table can be made up showing how much money each industry spends on purchases from each of the others.

The table, once constructed, can be used to follow chains of events through the economy. If building activity goes up, *all* the effects can be systematically followed by using the factors˙which distribute construction expenditures over each section of the economy. Of course, this is usually done by a computer rather than by actually tracing out effects on a chart, and there is a variety of factors which makes the practice of I-O modeling somewhat more complex than the simple picture described above. For instance, technical changes influence expenditures. If a new, cheap plastic wallboard is developed, the builders' expenditures on plywood will probably drop while those on plastics will increase. But several successful projects have developed working I-O models which are accessible to industrial and business planners at reasonable cost. These models have been discussed in more detail by the author* and in the references given in the Bibliography.

Markov Chains

Another model often encountered in discussions of forecasting is the Markov chain. This is a very neat idea, and the associated mathematics are quite interesting. Many quantities, especially in marketing, are the net results of import and export processes, or creation and destruction processes,

---

* Benton, W. K., *The Use of the Computer in Planning*, Addison-Wesley, Reading, Mass., 1971.

or other opposing forces. For example, when a new brand of consumer product is introduced, all users of that product are potential customers. Some of these actually switch to the new brand. Other remain with their old brands for longer or shorter periods. After the new brand is established, it continues to get new customers, but at a lower rate than at first. There are two reasons for this: (1) the size of the potential customer pool decreases, and (2) some present customers "switch out" to another brand.

These two processes oppose the effect of people "switching in" from the pool of noncustomers, and to some extent cancel it out. Given the market size, if the probabilities that noncustomers will switch in and present customers will switch out are known (and if the probabilities don't change), then the whole marketing history of the product can be forecast by using the known statistical facts about processes of this type, which are in fact Markov chains.

Technically, a Markov chain is characterized by a number of "states," such as "customer" and "noncustomer," and the probabilities of switching from any state to any other in a fixed time increment. There may be as many states as you like: "Brand A customer," "Brand B customer," "Brand C customer," and so on almost ad infinitum. No matter how many states you have, Markov theory postulates that there is always a final, stable number of people (or other elements) in each state. Eventually, that is, the number switching into a state equals the number switching out.

Many attempts to use Markov chains in market forecasting have been made. The concept has proved extremely valuable as a communications device and organizer of thought, but poor as an actual forecasting technique. More detailed dicussions can be found in the references given later.

Exercise. How much similarity is there between the I-O model and the Markov model? They both describe processes which allocate the contents of one box in an array over a line or column in the array, to produce a "later" version of the array. Are they identical? Can you restate a given I-O model as a Markov process? Can you restate a given Markov chain as an I-O process?

Technological Forecasting

Forecasts based on the past alone can be very useful in some situations, but to develop a truly useful input-output table, or even Markov chains in certain areas, you need to do another type of forecasting. This is forecasting changes in the way things are done; "technological forecasting" means forecasting facts about technology, *not* using technology to do forecasting.

The need for technological forecasting as part of input-output studies is obvious. Suppose, for example, that someone invents a plastic engine block for automobiles. Then the fraction of auto industry expenditures on plastics will increase while the fraction for steel will drop, and these changes must be reflected in the tables for the years following the invention.

All of this means that some method of forecasting inventions would be very useful, and in fact is crucial if input-output forecasts are to mean anything. Two or three techniques have been used to attempt technological forecasting, and the results seem to be much better than guesswork alone.

The first group of techniques are all variations on the "ask the experts" theme. One industrial input-output development project, for example, has panels of research scientists report, formally and regularly, on promising laboratory ideas, and speculate on the likely effects of future development of those ideas. When you stop to think that the principles of radar and television were well-known laboratory phenomena in the 1920's—although radar was not actually developed until World War II began in 1939 and television wasn't commercially exploited until five or ten years later—this method seems much more reasonable than it may at first. If a laboratory-to-factory lag of 20 to 30 years is typical, then we should be able to make pretty good educated guesses 20 or so years into the future, on the basis of present laboratory work.

The development cycle has actually speeded up considerably since the introduction of radar and television—and, of course, their 20-year cycle was faster than the cycles for the steam engine, the telephone, and the internal combustion engine. If you assumed that this speedup was part of the overall process, you could actually graph the trend in development times, and thus be able to predict the interval between major developments in each field. This would be useful in foretelling the likely duration of new technological arrangements

(Of course, we may have reached a climax in quick production. Several new products—thalidomide, cyclamates, and late-model cars—have been recalled from the market for defects that might have been exposed by a longer pre-market development and testing cycle. The growth of consumerism, also known as Naderism, may force a number of industries to return to more leisurely schedules. But that takes us into sociological prediction, far beyond the scope of this book.)

At any rate, the experts can at least give us clues. Of course, they never agree. Almost by definition, a group of researchers in any field will have different ideas about what is important and what can be done; if they didn't they would be talking about engineering rather than research. It is necessary, therefore, to determine the common basis of agreement in their diverse trains of thought. Techniques have been developed to do this, including one called the Delphi process, but they are extremely controversial. It is hard to tell whether the results are any better than those of ordinary panel discussions. In fact, it is hard to figure out just what the Delphi technique is, and I will therefore not attempt to describe it.*

An alternative to calling conferences of experts, which can be expensive as well as frustrating, is to graph the key characteristics of some technology-related process from year to year. For instance, airplane technology has changed a great deal since the Wright brothers' first flight, but every change has been reflected in the cost of flying a passenger one mile. So you can make a graph of cost per seat-mile (or ton-mile, or any other measure aircraft people might think appropriate) and use it to forecast future costs on the same basis. These future costs should then give you an idea of the timing and impact of future changes. The future changes will obviously be related to new technology, and unfortunately this method does not tell us what the technology will be. Experts might be able to guess, given the results of such a graph. But even without knowing the specific nature of the change we can benefit: We will not, for instance, build a giant new plant for the old process if all the signs point to a revolutionary new technique around the corner.

This graphing technique has been extensively applied to both the computer and the aircraft industries; both are highly dependent on technology and require large investments. The regularity of change in cost and performance over the years is striking, and forecasts based on the graphs are quite believable. They are not, of course, as useful in designing input-output tables as specific-invention forecasts would be. They cannot tell you what changes to expect in the purchases of the aircraft and computer industries. But they do tell you what other industries can expect to pay for air transportation and EDP, and provide a very useful check on simple extrapolations of dollar amounts.

Obviously caution is required in the use of such forecasts, no matter how suggestive the graphs may be, or how enthusiastic the researchers are about a new idea. New technology is intimately involved with a mass of ordinary business decisions as well as the changing tastes of consumers, and

---

* If you wish to grapple with the problem, see Wills, Ashton, and Taylor (eds.), *Technological Forecasting and Corporate Strategy*, American Elsevier, New York, 1969.

is therefore a highly complex subject. Nevertheless, though the results of work like this are not perfect, they are certainly better than forecasts of tomorrow's economy based on today's technology would be.

DEVELOPING A FORECASTING MODEL

The key element in developing a forecasting model, simulation or otherwise, is not the ability to deal with computers. Nor, despite the proponents of Markov and similarly complex models, is an advanced degree in statistics or mathematics required. The essential element is an *understanding* of the process you are trying to forecast. The use of a computer to carry out arithmetic or more detailed mathematics, and to "remember" the complexities of various interrelationships, is really incidental to the discovery of those relationships.

For instance, in the hospital data center example, all items of expense had to be estimated and accounted for. One of the items was salaries; it was necessary to estimate the cost of salesmen, programmers, and analysts. For this estimate to be realistic, it had to be done by people familiar with the field. Equally important, the entrepreneurs had to know that the timing of these expenditures was significant: that salesmen would be needed early in the venture, that each new customer would require the services of a conversion specialist for a given amount of time, and that customer representatives would have to be available continuously even after conversion. The same was true of equipment costs; facts on the basic cost of a terminal and a central computer could easily be obtained, but it required a little thought to relate those costs to the number of customers each salesman could be expected to bring in over a period of time, relate that information to the salesmen's salaries and arrive at an optimum number of salesmen, and finally bring all these factors and others together into an expected rate of growth.

Once the understanding is arrived at, converting it into a computer program is essentially a routine job. It does require specialists, but these correspond to the construction gang on a building site, not to the architect. Most of the failures in forecasting by computer models have resulted from leaving too much to the technicians. The man who has always built log cabins will build your next skyscraper out of Douglas fir if you let him, while another type will build you an elegant rustic retreat of stainless steel.

The only exception to the argument for keeping the technicians out of the initial design stages occurs when sufficient understanding is not available in the beginning and can only be supplied by research. Mathematicians and management specialists can be of great help in gathering data, and computers can be used advantageously to process them into understandable form. (This, again, is discussed in more detail in *The Use of the Computer in Planning*.) But this research essentially comes before the design phase, as programming comes after it. The design phase must always exist, even where is may not be obviously isolated, and thought must be given to it if the model is to succeed.

The real-estate forecasting examples can also serve to illustrate these points, but they also present other lessons for forecasters. The San Francisco simulation was chosen as an example primarily because it illustrates several important points very clearly:

1. Developing a forecasting simulation model of even a moderately complex social and economic process may be extremely expensive and time consuming; it may in fact be impossible. The lesson to be learned is that limited objectives should be chosen if simulation forecasting is to be done most effectively.

2. On the other hand, this model proves that relatively complex social and economic processes can actually be modeled in a $_r$ational way. The fact that something is difficult does not mean that it should never be attempted, although the expense involved does tend to keep large-scale simulations in the realm of research at present. However, the added detail they offer, in contrast to heuristics or other simple models, makes them a very practical management tool in some areas, such as flood control.

3. Problems of communication, interpersonal relationships, and general management are as important in the development of forecasting systems as they are in other facets of organization life. Even a magnificent job like the San Francisco simulation model can be totally ignored by those who could use it if they either don't understand it or don't have confidence in it.

The simpler BASS heuristic forecasting model demonstrates the practicality of compromise. This model is far less detailed than the San Francisco simulation, but the fact that it is easily comprehensible and fairly straightforward probably makes up for this lack of detail. For instance, it is certainly an aid in dealing with the third point mentioned above: communication among different groups of people. In practical forecasting situations, the heuristic approach is most often better than the detailed simulation, if for no other reason than this.

In general, the man who is building a forecasting model should approach the job as an architect, rather than as an engineer. He should give equal weight to understand the forces at work (so that he can model them) and to the needs and concerns of the groups who will be using his forecasts (so that he can be responsive as well as technically correct). If the forecaster can do a good job on these basic aspects of the job, the bricks and mortar will generally fall into place by themselves.

CHAPTER 3

CORRELATION AND REGRESSION

Forecasting methods based on relationships between the factor to be forecast and the variables in its environment are called relational methods. Simulation and heuristic models, discussed in the preceding chapter, make use of *known* relationships among variables. Correlation and regression, the subjects of this chapter, are used to *determine* relationships—whether they exist and, if so, what they are—so that forecasts can be made from them.

Unlike simulation and heuristic models, which are often quite complex, correlation and regression use only a single, simple, standardized type of relationship. However, even a simple forecasting formula can be very useful if it sorts out the variables that *actually* influence the dependent variable from all those that *might* influence it—and that is just what correlation and regression are designed to do.

An example may make the problem more vivid. Most competitive businesses experience frequent price changes, which may be influenced by many factors. Elementary economic theory, for instance, suggests that supply and demand determine prices. Can we be more precise, and actually use this concept to forecast price changes before they occur? Supply of a product can often be measured by tons of capacity, crop sizes, and other economic indices. Demand is not so easy to measure, since it doesn't come in tons or linear feet, but dollar measures can be devised: changes in personal income, for example, or investment decisions by manufacturers. The building products example described at the end of this chapter uses the number of building permits issued as such a "leading indicator" of demand. But finding appropriate measures of supply and demand only begins to attack the problem. There are many alternative detailed versions of the general idea; for example, the simple economic theory does not say whether it is the difference (supply minus demand) between the two factors, their ratio (demand divided by supply), or some other relationship that is significant. (Question: Which should be used?) Nor does it say anything about the effect of the general state of the economy, nor price (or supply or demand) increases or decreases in competing products. Thus what may at first look like a simple problem is actually far from it. In any given business a dozen different factors may be suspected of influencing prices. Any means of isolating and measuring the influence of the factors that actually are influential is a valuable management tool.

There are several steps in evaluating a suspected relationship. First, you need evidence that there *is* a relationship; the correlation concept provides a simple way of quantifying relations. The second step is to evaluate the evidence, to see whether it actually proves anything; a couple of technical tricks, the key portions of regression analysis, are used to do this. And the third step, by far the easiest, is to actually make forecasts based on the proven relationships.

Exercise 1. List ten factors which may be related to price changes in a business you are familiar with. Obtain as many measurements as possible of each factor over the past few years, and typical product prices at corresponding times; you should have at least 25 measurements of each factor you use. Then, as you read the rest of this chapter, imitate the analyses using your own real data to determine which of the suspected relationships are actually influential.

Exercise 2. If your business is not subject to price fluctuation you may prefer to use data from the stock market. Choose a common stock and list ten factors which might influence its price. Obtain a list of past prices and corresponding values for your factors, and again use these figure to follow the analysis process.

The Role of the Computer

A good deal of arithmetic is involved in accomplishing the computations for correlation and regression. This chapter does not contain derivations of the various formulas involved because they are a central subject of standard statistics texts and courses; there is no need for yet another version. And from the practical management point of view, it is not necessary to know the technical formulas at all. Even if a statistician is not available to assist in analyzing and modeling a given forecasting problem, nearly all computer systems today have programs to calculate these and other statistical quantities. Most of these programs have been used for several years by a variety of statistically sophisticated people and can be relied upon for accuracy and correctness. In most cases, use of these programs is free, although commercial services usually charge for the computer time involved in using them.

While it is not of crucial importance for the manager to develop extreme dexterity with calculation of these factors, it is important that he understand the concepts and processes of the computation, and that he understand the meaning of the results. This is especially true in view of the several different kinds of errors which can be made. Statistical relationships are not necessarily meaningful even if the arithmetic is correct, and not everything that comes out of a computer necessarily means what it seems to at first glance. A cautious attitude and an understanding of the principles of relational analysis can enable a forecaster to recognize and avoid most of these errors.

CORRELATION: THE BASIC IDEA

In seeking to discover whether there is a direct relationship between two series of values, the natural first question to ask is, "Do high values of one tend to be associated with high values of the other?", and the equivalent question for low values.

The simplest way to answer this question is called correlation. It directly compares high values and low values of the two factors, but some preliminary statistical steps are necessary. For instance, the word "high" really means "high relative to the average." Therefore we must find the average for each set of numbers, and then subtract it from each value.

Once this is done, the series of numbers representing each factor contains both positive and negative values. If the variables are correlated, positive values of one should be associated with positive values of the other, and negative values with negative values. Mixed positive-negative pairs will be less common.

Another statistical maneuver makes the correlation (or lack of it) easier to see. Multiplying two numbers which are either both positive or both negative gives a positive result. If there is a relationship between the two factors, most of the products will be positive, and so will their sum. The result is negative only for a mixed pair. If there is no relationship, about half of the products will be positive and about half negative, so their sum will be near zero. This sum, adjusted for the size of the variations, measures the relationship between the two factors directly. It is called the *correlation*, and is usually denoted R. If the two factors need to be named, they are customarily placed as subscripts to the R, as in $R_{x,y}$.

A mathematical series is usually said to have a total of N members, N meaning "a number," and any individual number between 1 and N is called I. The two series we have been talking about can be described by $X(1) \ldots X(N)$ and $Y(1) \ldots Y(N)$, and their averages are AVGX and AVGY. The two series of deviations from the average we produced are DX(I) and DY(I). None of this notation is vital to understanding, but it makes it easier to read and work with expressions like $DX(I) = X(I) - AVGX$.

A second adjustment must usually be made before the two factors can validly be compared.   A relatively large deviation in one series may be numerically smaller than a relatively small deviation in the other.   Comparing the sales of a small company with the U.S. GNP, for example, would produce this situation.   So the actual values of $DX(I)$ and $DY(I)$ must also be compared to a measure of the total variability in the X and Y factors.

The measure usually chosen for this purpose is the standard deviation; any introductory statistics text will tell you how to get it.   The standard deviation is denoted SD, and the final, truly-comparable numbers are given the new designation Z and are called Z-scores.   The final steps in our adjustment are then to calculate

$$ZX(I) = DX(I)/SDX \quad \text{and} \quad ZY(I) = DY(I)/SDY.$$

Now we have two series of Z-scores, derived from the original values by adjusting them for average and variability.   The actual correlation, denoted R or CORR, can then finally be calculated by:

$$R = (ZX(1)*ZY(1)) + (ZX(2)*ZY(2)) + \cdots + (ZX(N)*ZY(N)) N.$$

For computer use this might be written as

$$CORR = \frac{SUM\ (DX(I)*DY(I))\ FOR\ I = 1\ TO\ N}{SDX*SDY*N}.$$

The correlation will be 1.0 if the two factors are 100% related; it will be 0.0 if there is no relationship.   High values of one may sometimes be related to low values of the other; the correlation will be less than zero in this case, and can be as low as -1.0, a perfect negative correlation.   An example might be GNP and unemployment; when GNP is high, unemployment should be low, and vice versa.

What Does It All Mean?

The only problem with these neat formulas is that the results are sometimes a bit hard to interpret in real life.   To illustrate, we can take two readily available and interesting numerical series, the Dow Jones Industrials Averages and the prices of IBM stock.   Figure 3–1 shows twenty-four weeks of these series graphed together.

A standard computer program was used to calculate the correlation of the two series.   The results are shown in Fig. 3–2.   Obviously, a great deal more than the simple correlation was produced by the computer program; in fact, it is a bit hard for the uninitiated nonstatistician to locate the simple correlation in the printout.   This situation is unfortunately common in nearly all dealings with technical people, whether they are statisticians, computer experts, or any other type.

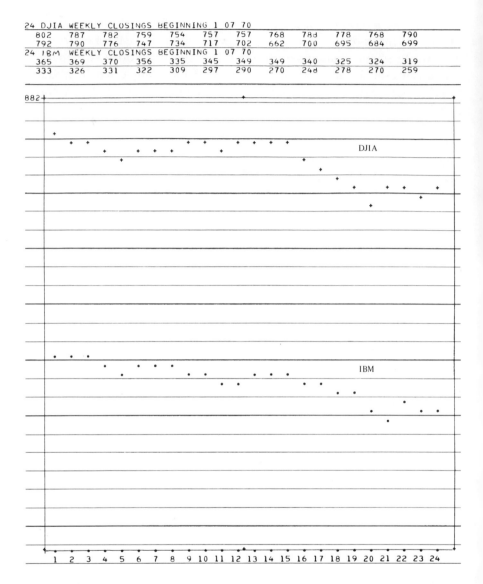

24 DJIA	WEEKLY	CLOSINGS	BEGINNING	1	07	70					
802	787	782	759	754	757	757	768	788	778	768	790
792	790	776	747	734	717	702	662	700	695	684	699

24 IBM	WEEKLY	CLOSINGS	BEGINNING	1	07	70					
365	369	370	356	335	345	349	349	340	325	324	319
333	326	331	322	309	297	290	270	248	278	270	259

Fig. 3–1 Weekly values of two correlated series, the Dow Jones Industrials Average (DJIA) and the price of IBM shares.

All of the results shown have meaning to a statistician. For our purpose the significant result is that the correlation is just over .85. This indicates a reasonably close relationship between IBM and DJIA. (Question: What does "reasonably close" mean?) As we sill see later, the factor R-SQUARED indicates what percentage of the variability in the first variable can be explained by its relationship to the second.

PROBLEM	IBM VS DJIA			
REGRESSION CASE	1			
DEPENDENT VARIABLE	1			

STANDARD ERROR OF Y	21.48660			
MULTIPLE CORRELATION	.85469			
R-SQUARED	.73049			
RES DEG OF FREEDOM	22			
SUM OF SQ RESIDUALS	1.01568E+04			
EXPLAINED VARIATION	2.75292E+04			
CONSTANT TERM	436.38116			

VARIABLE	BETA PRIME	BETA	SE(BETA)	STUDENT T
2	8.54686E-01	9.78624E-01	1.26732E-01	7.72199E+00

INVERSE CROSS-PRODUCT MATRIX
   3.47887E-05

ANALYSIS OF VARIANCE

TERM	SS	DF	MS
TOTAL	3.76860E+04	23	
REG	2.75292E+04	1	2.75292E+04
ERR	1.01568E+04	22	4.61674E+02

Fig. 3–2 Results of correlation analysis of data shown in Fig. 3–1. The main result is that there is a correlation R of slightly over 85% between the DJIA and the IBM price.

Some computer packages are designed in a more readable format, especially those provided on timeshared systems intended to be used by the relatively inexperienced person rather than the professional scientist. In general, however, it is wise to get all the results you can out of a computer run. The additional cost is negligible, and the additional data may very well clear up difficulties in interpreting the basic results. Any questions can then be taken to an expert together with the more complete printout.

If the results are to be presented to nonspecialists who need to grasp the essentials of the result, the extra information should be removed, of course. But retyping a few numbers is generally preferable to having incomplete, indecipherable, or misleading results.

Evaluating the Correlation Number

Once the calculations have been done, by computer or by hand, the forecaster is faced with a number between -1.0 and $+1.0$. He must decide what it means, and specifically how it can be used in forecasting. The main question that needs to be answered is: How likely is it that this correlation figure is the result of pure chance? If the number is based on a large number of data points and it is very large or very small, say above .75 or below −.75, it probably indicates a real association of values. If it is near 0.0, it probably indicates the absence of such association. But if it is in the middle ranges, say between .2 and .75, its significance is less clear.

The key to significance lies in the number of data points used. Correlations based on small numbers of points may vary widely, even if the underlying-population from which the data were derived does not. An analogy may help make this clear: the number of telephone calls a typical individual receives in a day varies quite widely. If three days are chosen at random and the number of telephone calls is averaged, there is a good chance that the average will be quite erroneous. But if the number of calls on 100 days is averaged, the actual number of telephone calls received per day will probably be estimated quite accurately. By analogy, a correlation based on a few points is likely to be quite inaccurate, while one based on a large number of points is reliable.

In practical forecasting, most work needs to be done in the gray area where there are between 10 and 50 data values. This is partly because business and government records are not often available for more than a few years, at least not records of what you are interested in. And this in turn is related to the fact that conditions change, so that older data are often irrelevant. The result is that in the real world forecasting is usually done in situations in which random errors are entirely possible, and they must be dealt with. The forecaster does this by "testing the null hypothesis."

The Null Hypothesis

To test the significance of a calculated correlation coefficient, the forecaster plays devil's advocate: He begins by saying, "The correlation may be due to pure chance." This supposition is called the *null hypothesis*. If there is a reasonably high chance that the calculated correlation number is the result of accidental variation, with no actual relationship between the two factors, the forecaster accepts the null hypothesis; that is, he concludes that the calculated R-value is an accident, and not meaningful. On the other hand, if the chance that the observed R-value could be accidental is very small, he can reject the null hypothesis and in effect conclude that there is a real relationship.

Two refinements are necessary to make this idea into a practical tool. First, the phrase "very small" must be made precise. This is usually done by choosing a percentage figure, usually one or five percent, depending on how strict a test is required. Second, the range of R-values that might be the result of accident must be established. This range will depend on the number of data points and on the percentage chosen; the method by which it is determined is shown pictorially in Fig. 3–3, and the details are spelled out in most statistics texts. Tables of ranges can also be found in texts and handbooks. The significant point here is that values *outside* the range will be interpreted as *non*accidental. (Question: Will the range become wider or narrower as the number of data points increases?)

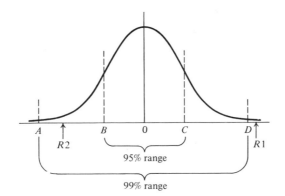

Fig. 3–3 Normal curve describing the distribution of R-values based on N data pairs where there is actually no correlation in the underlying populations. Ninety-five percent of the calculated values based on random choices of N points lie between points B and C; 99% lie between A and D. A value equal to R2 here is significant at the 95% level; R1 is significant at the 99% level. Actually, a modification of the R-value called T is used to get a truly normal distribution; see page 107 for the details.

In short, the statistician asks whether his calculated correlation number could reasonably be the result of accident, by comparing it to the values which are known to be accidentally possible. If his value is not in the range which includes 95%, 99%, or some other percentage of the "accidental" values, the calculated R-value is said to be "significant at" the specified percentage. (Question: Suppose your calculated R is significant at the 95% level. Could it still be accidental? What is the probability?)

With a large number of data points, where there actually is no correlation, there may be only a 1% chance of calculating a correlation over .90. A value of .91 is then extremely unlikely to be the result of chance alone, so the forecaster can conclude that this value is meaningful. For a smaller number of data points, there may be a 10% chance of finding an accidental correlation over .90. A value of .91 is then less certain to be meaningful, and the forecaster will probably conclude that it cannot be used. For this same situation, however, there may be only a 1% chance of calculating a correlation of over .98. A correlation of .99 is therefore meaningful ("at the 1% level").

These values are only examples. Actually, the values are different for every different number of data points used. The fewer data points there are, the more chance there is of getting a high correlation value by accident. If you try to pick the Queen of Spades out of a shuffled deck of cards, your chance is $1/52$, but if you want to do it five times running the figure is $1/52^5$: one chance in about 380 million as opposed to one in 52. The same sort of odds applies to correlations, but even more dramatically: If only four data points are used, it can be proven that any correlation is as likely as any other. For four data points, then, *any* correlation value is meaningless. The situation improves gradually as the number of data points increases, so that when there are more than 25 data points any value over .75 is probably meaningful.

In general, then, the method of dealing with the possibility of accidental correlations is:

1. Choose a level of significance, often 5%.

2. Calculate (or find in a statistical table) the correlation value which is exceeded that percentage of the time, assuming that there is no actual correlation.

3. Compare the calculated value R with this test value. If R exceeds the test value, it is meaningful. Otherwise there is a good chance that it is purely an accident, and it should not be interpreted as indicating a real relationship.

Some Pitfalls of Correlation

Correlation is technically infallible. If high values of one variable are associated with high values of another, the correlation between them will work out to a high number, generally between .8 and 1.0. But while this is mathematically significant, it is not always so in real life. One problem is that if both the factors are growing or declining as time passes, the correlation coefficient will always be high, even if there is no traceable relation between the factors themselves. This means that the correlation between almost any economic measures in the last twenty years, for instance, will be very high.

In his preliminary investigations of the paper market in Brazil, a paper manufacturer obtained publicly available data on sales of various types of paper and on the Brazilian gross national product (GNP). He then used a computer program to find the correlations among all these factors. Not surprisingly, since both the GNP and the paper industry have been growing, all the correlations turned out quite high. Some are shown in Fig. 3–4. Interpreting these figures is a difficult task because they are all so close to 1.

Correlation matrix

	1	2	3	4
1. GNP	1.00	.95	.91	.92
2. Total paper consumption		1.00	.97	.99
3. Kraft paper consumption			1.00	.98
4. Bleached paper consumption				1.00

Fig. 3–4 Sample correlations among segments of the Brazilian paper market and the overall Brazilian economy. The table entries are the calculated correlations between each pair of factors; for example, the correlation between total paper consumption and bleached paper consumption is shown as 99%. The very high correlations actually reflect consistent growth in all of the factors studied rather than particularly close interdependence, and may be misleading. Techniques for dealing with this spuriously close relationship are discussed in the text.

One solution to this problem is to look at the second significant digit, dismissing the initial ".9" as a mere reflection of the long-term growth. The second digit varies more widely, and in fact does reflect differences in co-variability of the various factors.

A more useful solution is suggested by the graph in Fig. 3–1. Not only do the DJIA and the price of IBM's stock both tend in general to decline over the period shown, but smaller variations are reflected in both. If those smaller variations could be measured and *their* correlation calculated, the resulting figure would probably be more meaningful. In fact, it is quite easy to do. All that is needed is to draw a straight line through the two sets of factors and subtract the long-term trend value from the actual value. The specific method for drawing the line will be discussed later. The resulting residual values of both series can then be correlated to provide a more meaningful index of the relationship. This method can also be illustrated graphically, whereas the second-digit method cannot easily be pictured.

Another source of arithmetically real but actually meaningless correlation figures are data with cyclical variation. If both factors move up and down cyclically, and the cycle lengths are not greatly different, there will be apparent correlation over any fairly short time period. This situation is illustrated in Fig. 3–5; it arises in the real world in connection with inventory levels, commodity prices, stock prices, and so on. One of the interesting habits of spurious correlations due to cycles is the tendency for the calculated and apparently significant correlation to change as different time periods are studied—thus providing a favorite source of academic disputes.

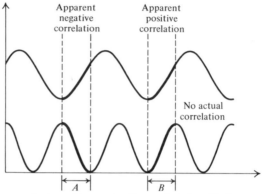

Fig. 3–5 Apparent correlation of two actually unrelated cyclical processes. As long as the observations period is relatively short and the cycle lengths are not radically different, a high correlation coefficient is likely to result from cyclical data. The calculated coefficient, however, will change radically as different observation periods are used, such as A and B in this graph.

The forecaster must be aware of these problems with correlations, and in specific cases should try to see that they do not influence his work.

REGRESSION: ANOTHER WAY OF LOOKING AT IT

Correlation simply compares the frequency with which high values of one variable are associated with high values of another. The picture most appropriate for dealing with correlations is a graph showing both series of values in parallel. But another type of picture is more common when we are dealing with the effect of one variable on another. It is the *Cartesian* graph used in high-school geometry, where dependent values like $(X/2) + 1$ and X^2 are plotted against the values of the independent variable X. Each point on the graph has a horizontal distance equal to X and a vertical distance equal to the dependent variable's value, as in Fig. 3–6.

The same kind of graph can be drawn for variables involved in forecasting. One variable must be regarded as the dependent variable; the others are viewed as independent variables. For instance, if a forecaster is trying to forecast IBM price from the DJIA, then the IBM price is the dependent variable and the DJIA value is the independent value. Each value of the DJIA specifies a horizontal distance to the point on the graph, and the IBM price specifies the point's height above the bottom of the graph.

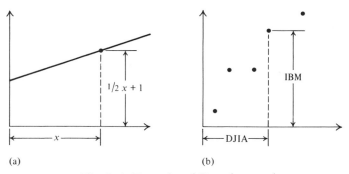

(a)   (b)

Fig. 3–6 Examples of Cartesian graphs.

A graph like this should show correlation quite clearly. If high values of the dependent variable are actually associated with high values of the independent variable, the points should form a trail which rises or falls from left to right. This notion is at the heart of regression analysis, a method which is more powerful than correlation analysis.

Figure 3–7 contains a graph in which the IBM price is the independent variable and the DJIA value is the dependent. The data are the same as in Fig. 3–1, simply graphed a different way. There is an obvious grouping about a line from lower left to upper right; low values and high values of both variables do seem to be associated. The forecaster's questions, as in the case of correlation, are:

"Is there any relationship?"

"How important is it? That is, how can we measure it numerically?"

"What is the chance that there really is no relationship, and the apparent relation is due to random variations?"

"Is there any other kind of accident involved?"

The Basic Idea

The answers to the questions above are very simple conceptually, although as usual a good deal of arithmetic is necessary to put the ideas into practice. The first step is to draw a straight line on the graph, coming as close as possible

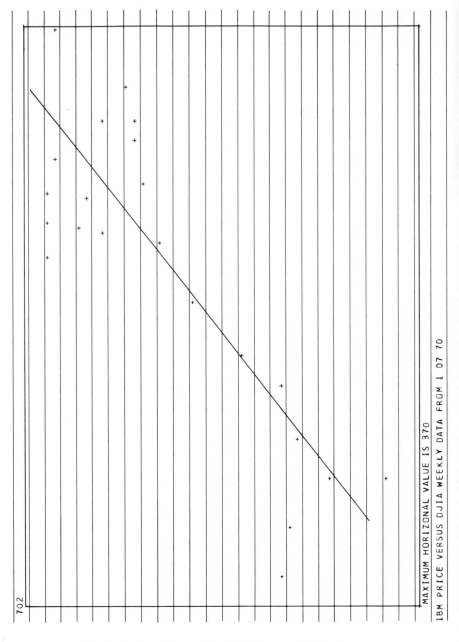

Fig. 3–7 Cartesian graph of DJIA versus IBM values.

to all the points. A good first try is shown in Fig. 3–7. Some routine methods in general use for finding the best line are described in the chapter on trends; this is generally done by means of a computer package.

If there actually is a relationship between the two variables, the fitted straight line will not be horizontal. It will exhibit some slope, and the size of the slope can be used to answer the third question above. If there are only a few data points, even a relatively large slope can be the result of random variation, while with a large number even a small slope is significant. The logic is the same as that for testing the significance of a correlation, and need not be repeated here.

Measuring the importance of the relationship, however, does require some new and valuable ideas. And here we begin to get into something directly related to forecasting.

One way to forecast the independent variable is simply to use the average value. Now, the average value can be compared to all of the known values, and a total error computed. This total error is simply the total of the distances from each data point to the average value, as shown in Fig. 3–8. At the same time, the values of the fitted line can be compared to the known values, and a total error for the fitted line can be computed. If the points really do form a line, the total error from the fitted line should be much smaller than the total error from the average. A comparison of the two totals can then be used as a numerical measure of the relationship.

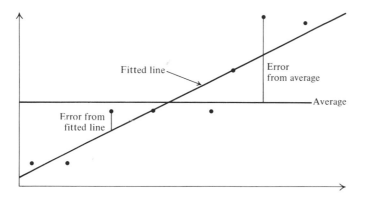

Fig. 3–8 Finding the average error.

The most obvious comparison of the two totals is their ratio. Suppose the total of the errors from the average is 100, and the total of the errors from the fitted line is 28. The ratio is then 28/100, or .28. A close relationship between the two variables is reflected in a small value of this ratio; a value of 1.0 reflects no relationship. This is the reverse of the way correlation figures come out; in correlation, zero indicates no relationship while a value near 1.0 represents a close relationship. For consistency, the regression ratio should be subtracted from one. In this example, the result would be a value of $1.00 - 0.28 = 0.72$. This regression coefficient now indicates a close relationship just as it would for correlation.

As in most statistical measurements, the arithmetic error is usually replaced by the square of the error so that negative and positive errors do not cancel each other out and produce totals near zero. Statisticians call the sum of the squared errors from the fitted line the residual sum of squares, and denote it SS. They call the sum of the squared errors from the average *the total sum of squares*, and denote this SST. The measure described above, using these error sums, is called the coefficient of determination:

$$\text{coefficient of determination} = 1 - (SS/SST).$$

The coefficient of determination varies from zero to one, and, just as with correlation, a value near zero indicates no relationship while a high value denotes strong relation. And just as with correlation, it is the values in between that cause the trouble.

Actually, the relationship between the correlation coefficient R and the coefficient of determination turns out to be closer than the general observation made above. It turns out to be so close, in fact, that it provides a symbol or common name for the coefficient of determination: R-squared. The value of the coefficient of determination, in other words, is the square of the correlation coefficient. Since the correlation coefficient is less than one, its square is smaller than itself. For example:

Correlation coefficient (R)	Coefficient of determination (R-squared)
.90	.81
.80	.64
.70	.49

The close relationship of R and R-squared is a little surprising unless the calculations that prove the relationship are studied. Then the formula for R and the formula for the coefficient of determination show the relationship quite clearly. In Fig. 3–2, R-squared was presented in the computer printout just after the correlation coefficient.

Another Viewpoint

The view of regression presented above depends on separating the total error into two parts, one being the distance from the data point to the regression line, and the other being the distance from the regression line to the average. The question then was, "Are the errors from the line much less than the errors from the average?" The same question can also be posed in a slightly different way: "What fraction of the total error (from the average) is contributed by the (slope of the) fitted line?"

If R-squared is .85, then the error from the fitted line is only 15% of the error from the average. Looking at this another way, use of the fitted regression line reduces the error by 85%. If high or low values of the independent variable actually do produce high or low values of the dependent variable, then a large part of the errors from the average are the result of variations which are related to changes in the independent variable. And R-squared tells you what fraction of the total error this is. In our example, 85% of the total error is the result of variations produced by the relationship between the dependent and the independent variable.

Statisticians usually express this by saying, "The independent variable explains (so many) percent of the total variation," or "The regression reduces the total error by (so many) percent." In the case of the IBM–DJIA relationship, the DJIA explains about 73% of the variability in the IBM price. That is, the R-squared is 0.73.

Multiple Regression

In real-life management and planning, an important dependent variable is usually related to several independent variables. The price of a given stock next year may be related to its price this year, the average market level this year, the GNP, the discount rate, and a host of other possibilities. The net profit of a manufacturing firm may be related not only to gross sales but also to the number of employees, the average selling price, the inventory level of raw materials, the inventory level of manufactured pieces, and so on. This multiplicity of influences means that practical forecasting questions do not usually arise neatly in a form suitable for regression analysis. No one says, "What is the strength of the relationship between factor A and factor B?" A much more likely form is, "What the hell went wrong with our sales last month?"

Even when phrased in analytical terms, the real questions are likely to be less clear than the examples discussed so far. One of the most common of these genuine questions is, "Which of the factors we know about actually influences the results most? Which are so insignificant that we can disregard them? Is a rule-of-thumb guess, based on one indicator, just as good as a complex statistical forecast using regressions and correlations and computers and all that?"

Actually, regression itself can be used to answer this question, if facts are available on all the various factors. Suppose the thing we are trying to forecast is called factor X: It may be the price of a stock or the profitability of a division. Suppose a group of factors—A, B, C, . . .—all influence X to some degree, but we are not sure how important each of them is. If you are familiar with regression, the obvious first step is to find out how closely X is related to A, to B, and so on. This can be done either by correlation calculations, which produce R, or by regression calculations, which produce R-squared.

This sort of work involves an immense amount of calculation, and it is therefore usually done by computer. Assuming this method, the analysis can be done in a step-by-step fashion. The computer selects the single independent variable which accounts for the most variation in X; that is, it picks out the highest R-squared. Then it recalculates and selects the one which accounts for the most remaining variation, and so on. The really significant variables are usually identified in the first few steps, and those remaining have rather small effects. The computer program generally tests the significance of using further variables on the basis of the "Could it be accidental?" idea outlined earlier. If adding a given variable does increase the R-squared value, but by so small an amount that it is not statistically significant, the variable is not added to the list of explanatory factors.

Multiple regression can obviously become a very technical subject very quickly. There are many minor variations on the method; for instance, it is possible to fit a regression formula to the given data using all the variables at once. The result of this direct regression is a forecasting formula based on all the factors, and the forecaster must decide on the relative importance of each. The step-wise technique described above, while slower, does give the forecaster a bit more information, and presents it in the order of its importance.

Using Multiple Regression

Once the calculations have been done, the forecaster wants to use them to produce regular numerical forecasts. The first step in regression produces a straight line relating one variable to the dependent variable. This line can be written as an equation:

$X = A + B*C$, where C is the most important variable.

In a linear equation like this one, A is the value of Y where $X = 0$, and B is the rate at which Y increases, which is the slope of the line. In a multiple regression, however, things don't stop here. The second most important variable is identified, and must be added. If this second variable is denoted D, the new equation is:

$$X = A + B*C + B2*D.$$

Here the values of A and B differ from those in the first equation. And the process continues until there are no more significant variables. The result is an equation something like:

$$X = A + B*C + B2*D + B3*E + \cdots + BN*N.$$

The final values of A, B, B2, and so on to BN will again be different from those you started with, since each new variable you add modifies the influence of the previous ones. You can add variables indefinitely, as long as they increase the R-squared value, but four or five are usually enough. R-squared means exactly the same for several variables as for one, it is the ratio of errors from the calculated regression value to errors from the average, subtracted from one.

Having found the coefficients (A, B1, B2, and so on), the forecaster can put them into the general equation along with measurements of the significant factors (C, D, E, ..., N) to produce working forecasts. In the case of one corporate model, this approach was used to identify the factors affecting profit in each of the firm's divisions, so that profit forecasts could be made for the whole organization.*

The *F-statistic* or *F-test* is also likely to occur in discussions of regression. It is used in testing the significance of new variables in a regression analysis. In practical terms, the F-test tells you whether there is a real difference between a multiple regression using factors A, B, C, ..., M, and a second regression using all of these plus one more, say N. The key question, of course, is whether adding the extra variable really reduces the errors very much.

In technical terms, the F-statistic is the ratio of the variability of one population to the variability of another. For regression using the notation above, the two populations are (1) the errors based on regression without N,

---

* Gershefski, George W., "Building a Corporate Financial Model," *Harvard Business Review,* July–August 1969.

and (2) the errors based on regression using N. The statistic is the ratio of the variability of the first population to the variability of the second. If the two variabilities are the same, the ratio is 1.0 and the F-test indicates no difference between the populations. In other words, adding the extra variable doesn't make any difference. If the variabilities differ, the difference may or may not be significant. Significance, as in simple correlation, depends on the number of data-points involved, and the appropriate decision level for a given number of points in each population can be found in the large F-statistic tables that statisticians are fond of poring over.

In short, there are several things to look at in evaluating a multiple regression. The first is the R-squared value, which gives you a rough idea of how much your variables explain about the independent factor. You can compare the R-squared figures for different combinations of variables to pick out the most likely. The F-test then tells you precisely whether the improvement in R-squared resulting from adding a new variable is likely to be the result of chance, or whether it is in fact significant.

Figure 3–9 shows a sequence of regressions run on a time-sharing console. The first portion of the printout was produced while getting the regression program ready to use and entering the data; three regression analyses follow. In all three the dependent variable is the present price of IBM stock; the two independent variables are the IBM price and the DJIA value one week earlier. The first regression finds the relation between this week's IBM price and last week's DJIA (or, looking at it another way, between this week's DJIA and next week's IBM price). The correlation R is .89, which the F-statistic shows to be significant. The next run shows a closer relation between IBM price in successive weeks than between IBM and the previous week's DJIA, since the R-value is .93, and the F-statistic is correspondingly higher. The third run relates IBM to both values in the previous week, and provides a still higher R of .95248, also shown to be significant by a high F-value.

REGRESSION AND FORECASTING

Regression is obviously a useful tool for measuring a relationship, but not all relationships are useful in forecasting. The most obvious limitation is that the independent variable should be measured at some time preceding measurement of the independent variable if the regression equation is to be used for forecasting. What you need is a relationship between changes in the independent variable and *later* changes in the dependent variable. The

```
RUN S_***STATPACK

STATPACK    11:55   09/13/71   MONDAY      002


ARE YOU A STATPACK EXPERT
?* YES

FILE NAMES
?* BILL,*

ANALYSIS
?* MULT

READ FILE
?* NO

ROWS,COLUMNS
?* 802,365._,369_____3,__3,24

THAT IS TOO MANY.   THE MAXIMUM IS 15 COLUMNS.   TRY IT AGAIN.
?* 24,__3,3

NOW, ENTER EACH ROW
?8802,365,369
    ? ,_787,369,370,_
? 782,370,356
? 759,356,335
? 754,335,345
? 757,345,349
? 757,349,349
? 768,349,340
? 788,340,325
? 778,325,2_324
? 768,324,319
```

3. IBM price.
2. Last week's IBM price.
1. Last week's DJIA.

```
SPECIFY THE DEPENDENT VARIABLE
?* 3

NO. INDEP VAR
?| 1

SPECIFY THESE VARIABLES
? 1
                                    (Last week's DJIA)

VARIABLE    REG.COEF.    STD.ERROR COEF.    COMPUTED T    BETA COEF.
   1         0.77602        0.08675          8.94506       0.89000

INTERCEPT               -265.33081
MULTIPLE CORRELATION       0.89000    (ADJUSTED R =      0.89000)
STD. ERROR OF ESTIMATE    16.23599    (ADJUSTED SE=     16.23599)

                ANALYSIS OF VARIANCE FOR THE REGRESSION
     SOURCE OF VARIATION       D.F.   SUM OF SQ.    MEAN SQ.     F VALUE
ATTRIBUTABLE TO REGRESSION      1     21092.238    21092.238    80.014
DEVIATION FROM REGRESSION      21      5535.762      263.608
         TOTAL                 22     26628.000
```

Fig. 3–9 Sequence of regressions run on a timesharing console.

alternative is to produce independent forecasts of the value of the independent variables, but this is the long way around unless you have good reasons

```
MORE REGRESSION
?* YES

SPECIFY THE DEPENDENT VARIABLE
?* 3

NO. INDEP VAR
?* 1

SPECIFY THESE VARIABLES
?* 2
                                          (Last week's IBM price)
VARIABLE    REG.COEF.    STD.ERROR COEF.    COMPUTED T    BETA COEF.
   2          0.96914         0.07915         12.24388       0.93655

INTERCEPT                    5.34814
MULTIPLE CORRELATION         0.93655    (ADJUSTED R =    0.93655)
STD. ERROR OF ESTIMATE      12.48195    (ADJUSTED SE=   12.48195)

                  ANALYSIS OF VARIANCE FOR THE REGRESSION
        SOURCE OF VARIATION        D.F.    SUM OF SQ.     MEAN SQ.     F VALUE
ATTRIBUTABLE TO REGRESSION          1      23356.219     23356.219    149.912
DEVIATION FROM REGRESSION           21      3271.781       155.799
        TOTAL                       22     26628.000


SPECIFY THE DEPENDENT VARIABLE
?* 3

NO. INDEP VAR
?* 2

SPECIFY THESE VARIABLES
?* 1,2
                                              (Both)
VARIABLE    REG.COEF.    STD.ERROR COEF.    COMPUTED T    BETA COEF.
   1          0.30140         0.10829          2.78333       0.34567
   2          0.66712         0.12851          5.19105       0.64469

INTERCEPT                  -123.77997
MULTIPLE CORRELATION         0.95469    (ADJUSTED R =    0.95248)
STD. ERROR OF ESTIMATE      10.85888    (ADJUSTED SE=   11.11441)

                  ANALYSIS OF VARIANCE FOR THE REGRESSION
        SOURCE OF VARIATION        D.F.    SUM OF SQ.     MEAN SQ.     F VALUE
ATTRIBUTABLE TO REGRESSION          2      24269.695     12134.848    102.912
DEVIATION FROM REGRESSION           20      2358.305       117.915
        TOTAL                       22     26628.000

MORE REGRESSION
?* NO
```

Fig. 3–9 (contd.)

for believing in these forecasts.   Usually, independent forecasts of independent variables are useful when forecasting over long time spans, since trends in the independent variables are more likely to be important over long time periods.

Independent variables which change before the dependent variable does are called *leading indicators*, and play a central role in economic forecasting.   In the example given earlier in this chapter, the values of IBM stock price and DJIA in a given week were leading indicators of the price of IBM the following week.

The time element is important, but application of regression to real forecasting situations has more subtle dangers as well. The next exercise will show you a major one.

Exercise. Reread the section titled "Some Pitfalls of Correlation." Do the problems described there apply to regression as well? It was suggested that you might detect false correlations arising from simultaneous growth by correlating the differences between successive values; does this work for regression? What about spurious correlations resulting from mismatched cycle lengths?

Some forecasters take such a serious view of these problems that they reject all regressions except those in which the independent variables are mathematical formulas which cannot change "accidentally," or variables which have an obvious causal relationship.* The opposite approach, which allows use of any independent variables as long as they result in significant improvements in the regression, is sometimes referred to by stricter statisticians as the "kitchen sink" method.

Since the only thing that really matters is whether a given model produces better forecasts, the whole argument is slightly academic. A better regression fit does not guarantee better forecasts. The only way to find out whether a model using one set of variables produces better forecasts than another model with a different set of variables is to use the models to forecast values which are known, but were not used in model development. If model A produces better forecasts in simulated forecasting than model B, then the additional variables in it are significant to the forecaster. Even proponents of the kitchen sink method admit that the relationships which make the forecasts better may eventually change, so that a revised model will become necessary. There are no immutable truths in forecasting.

As a result, it is best to develop a regression model using one group of data, and then to test the model by simulating forecasts of a second group of data which does not overlap with the first. Usually the two data groups are from different time periods—the first half of the data points for developing regressions and the second half for testing them as forecasting tools. The process can be viewed as a cycle of developing hypotheses, testing the ones that look most promising, and then going back to develop more promising

---

* The case for this view is stated in Brown, R. G., *Smoothing, Forecasting, and Prediction of Discrete Time Series*, Prentice-Hall, Englewood Cliffs, N.J., 1962.

ones. The hypotheses are relations between independent variables and the dependent ones; they are developed by a series of refinements. The first step in developing the hypothesis is to look for rough correlations, for suggestions among the causes known to be involved. Then the rough results of this first step can be refined by using regressions instead of correlations, and using the F-statistic to test the significance of each added variable. The F-test guards against spurious relationships due to pure random variation, but the professional statistician can also use several other tests, including the Durbin-Watson statistic, to weed out spurious correlations due to other causes.

Having developed a regression model in which all the terms appear to be reasonable and significant, the forecaster then tests it by producing forecasts for each point in the second set of data. He compares the simulated values to the real ones, perhaps using a picture like that suggested at the end of Chapter 4. He searches for consistent errors: overestimation, too-early anticipation of changes, and the like. And then he goes back to the first part of the process. He may, for instance, try out the difference between two independent variables as a new independent variable, or use the square or the logarithm of one of them in an attempt to correct the faults he has observed. His imagination is his only guide. If he can improve the fit, measured by the R-squared and evaluated by the F-statistic and others, he is ready for further tests of the newly improved hypothesis.

Making Sense out of Price Changes

One of my colleagues was once hired by an international trade association to help them forecast the prices they should expect to get. The association's members produced a widely-used commodity, made in large quantities in several countries and sold throughout the world. Both supply and demand in this commodity changed rapidly, and prices therefore fluctuated widely. But there always seemed to be a cause for each price change. When the price fell, the association could look backward and see, perhaps, that a new synthetic competing with their commodity had recently reduced its price, or perhaps that the quantity produced had increased greatly, leading to a glut. If the price of their commodity rose, they might look back again and see that there had been a shortage or a price increase in a substitute material, so that their market was larger than usual. A number of different products competed with the commodity, and other factors such as style changes also affected the outcome.

The association's economists wondered if these cause-and-effect relationships could be captured in a form that would enable the association to look ahead and predict prices, rather than look backward and try to explain them after they had occurred. They presented the problem to the forecasting expert in the form of a challenge. They asked, in effect, "Can you find a way to predict the price of our commodity one year in advance, with an error that is less than one percent at least 95 % of the time?" The forecaster was the kind of man who liked a challenge. He replied that he didn't know whether he could, but that he would like to try.

The association had lots of data about prices and almost all the possibly-related factors they could think of. The statistician's job was essentially to plunge in and try to make sense out of it all. The tool he chose was regression, in conjunction with a timeshared computer console.

Using Timesharing

Timesharing is one of the more glamorous approaches to computer use, and in some cases it can be the most practical. Instead of using a specific block of time on your firm's computer or at a service bureau, you can sit at a terminal, usually a typewriter-like console, and communicate with the computer over telephone wires without any delays. You can type in commands ordering the machine to perform this regression or find that correlation, wait a few seconds for the machine to do its work, and then have the results printed out in front of you. If you are not satisfied with the answer, you can then try something else, just by repeating the procedure. This is in strong contrast to the hours you might spend at a service bureau or even your own company's computer installation, "waiting for turnaround," and the magic is accomplished at a low enough price for practical use by having the machine service a large number of users at once. The work isn't really done simultaneously, but the few split-seconds the machine spends on somebody else's program before getting to yours hardly matters to a human user, and by sharing both the time available and the cost of the central computer many users can do more work at less cost.

In the case of the trade association, the statistician loaded the data that looked most promising into his computer files. Then he worked in his office, using the terminal to try out ideas and test hypotheses without the tedium of doing extensive calculations himself, supervising a group of clerks, or waiting for a large "batch processing" computer to do his regressions. In this way he was able to evaluate the effects of competitive products' prices, variations in supply and demand (which were measured, for example, by disposable income in the major consuming countries), and other factors without wasting a great deal of time on the tedious tasks usually needed to get a regression analysis done. For two or three months the statistician alternately worked feverishly at his computer console and pored over the results—R-squareds and F-tests—at his desk.

The final result was a triumphant failure. The statistician found that he could not come within the one percent target using the data available to him, although he could come within five percent. That was pretty good. The final forecasting equation was a regression involving half a dozen terms, some of them ratios of prices and quantities. Each term had been proven significant by the F-test. A very large number of hypotheses had been tested, tinkered with, and rejected by the same test.

Not one percent of the work that went into this project could have been done without a computer. And the timesharing terminal made using the computer about as easy as driving a car. The combination of regression analysis programs and timeshared computers has led to a real explosion in the use of this forecasting method. As this example shows, there is good reason for it.

Some Reservations about Timesharing

What makes timesharing valuable in forecasting is that it gives the forecaster the ability to try a variety of approaches and models quickly and easily. A highly experienced forecaster can interpret the R's, F's, and so on very quickly, and often knows as soon as the results are printed which direction he wants to move in. The beginner, or the man with a different temperament, is not so fortunate. He may need to stew over the results of a run before he is ready to try again. And he *should* think over his preliminary results before he goes on to produce more. Even the expert who carried out the price forecasting analysis, a consultant in a leading research organization, found that he spent more time in his office mulling over the computer's most recent calculations than he did at the computer console. Most companies' computer centers, and nearly all commercial service bureaus, can produce a regression analysis overnight. Most can produce a run during the course of a few hours if you are in a rush. The price is about half that of timesharing—and less if it is your own company's machine.

The important thing is not the computer technology, timeshared or teleprocessed or whatever. What solves problems is imaginative development of regression hypotheses and thoughtful interpretation of the results. To some extent, the timeshared terminal can interfere with this reflection because it is there, waiting to be used. Pushing buttons can be much more fun than thinking carefully. The temptation should be resisted.

The real advantage of a timeshared terminal is that you can use it without leaving your office. And that also may or may not be an advantage, depending on your temperament, the climate in which you are located, and the number of telephone calls and other interruptions that are likely to occur in your office. A service bureau's client room can be a very pleasant, private place to think while you wait for your results.

Autocorrelation

There are a number of variations on the general theme of regression. One of these is to treat each past value of a variable as if it were itself a separate variable. In fact, all of the past values can be treated as a series of variables. If $X(T)$ represents a series of values of X as T (time) varies, the individual values can be represented:

Dependent variable (that is, the present value) $= X(T)$
First independent variable (value last time) $= X(T - 1)$
Second independent variable (value time before last) $= X(T - 2)$
and so on.

The dependent variable can then be regressed against each of the potential independent variables to determine how closely the value of X depends on the previous values. If the time intervals are monthly, $T - 12$ represents data one year ago, and regression of X on $X(T - 12)$ will show up any annual or season effects that may be present. For instance, beach umbrellas and snow tires will have high R-squared values for $T - 12$ and possibly $T - 11$ and $T - 13$. Other intervals can, of course, be chosen to test other cyclical effects.

In general it is just as useful to regard this procedure as a correlation rather than a regression. In this case, the value of R for each time unit (or delay, represented by D) indicates the strength of the recurrence factor for that unit. Each calculation relating $X(T)$ to $X(T - D)$ is called an *autocorrelation*.

For instance, a garment manufacturer found that the demand for his fashion line was closely correlated with disposable income over the long term, say, several years. But in shorter periods of a few months sales often showed violent fluctuations. Autocorrelation analysis carried out by the company forecaster showed significant negative autocorrelation between $X(T)$ and $X(T - D)$, the value of a few months earlier. In plain English, short-term dips in sales were offset several months later by increased sales, as consumer demand forced retailers to replenish inventories. The analyst was able to design a useful forecasting method for future sales based on both the long-term trend and the short-term fluctuations. Although the system was abstract and mathematical, it apparently reflected periodic waves of optimism and pessimism that sweep the garment industry, as well as accidental combinations of retail inventory management decisions, and it did so successfully enough to be quite useful.*

Practical Uses in Credit and Sales

Regression is generally regarded as a means of determining the cause or causes of some effect, or at least of distinguishing the relative importance of the various possible causes. Statisticians, however, are always careful to specify that regression does not identify causes, but only measures relationships. This disclaimer is important because a relationship may reflect the fact that both factors are actually caused by ("related to") a third, and because the existence of a relationship doesn't tell you which factor causes which. Medieval scientists believed that rotting meat "caused" flies because the two were invariably associated. There are several famous stories in which regression indicated a relationship which was misinterpreted as cause and effect. The apparent relation of two cyclic factors discussed earlier in this chapter is one such example.

Careful observation and a few experiments succeeded in disproving the theory of "spontaneous generation of life" that was built on the meat and the flies, and they should do the same for any misinterpretations that creep into your use of regression. Once you have learned to be pragmatic and apply appropriate tests, regression can be used very constructively. The following examples show cases in which the cause-and-effect interpretation causes no difficulty, where the results are clear, and, most important, where regression is obviously more effective than alternate methods.

Banks, savings and loan associations, and consumer goods retailers all extend credit to individual customers. In fact or in effect, they lend people money. But they will not lend to every individual who asks. They must first determine that the applicant has a sufficiently high probability of paying the loan back.

Stripped of the banking industry's phrasing, then, the loan officer's basic function is to forecast a given applicant's probability of repayment. He usually has several items of information about the individual to help him decide: sex, age, health, marital status, number of children, ownership of a house or car, and so on. He may also have other items which experience in certain areas has shown to be important, such as whether or not the appli-

---

* For more details, see Magee, John R., and David M. Boodman, *Production Planning and Inventory Control*, 2nd ed., McGraw-Hill, N.Y., 1967, p. 104.

cant has a telephone and what kind of music he prefers. Again phrasing in terms of regression, he has a list of independent variables.

The dependent variable, the desirability of the account, may be measured in a number of ways. You might count the number of days delay in payment over a given period, or the percentage of the loan that is eventually paid back or paid back on time. No matter which he chooses, the officer's basic problem is to determine the comparative importance of his independent variables (the applicant's characteristics) in relation to the dependent variable (the applicant's desirability). In other words, which characteristic or characteristics will tell him, most often and accurately, whether the applicant will pay up? Better yet, the officer may hope to discover a formula for determining how desirable this applicant is in relation to other applicants, using the characteristics that have been found to be significant. If this applicant ranks high on characteristics A and D, is he a better or worse prospect than someone who ranks high on B and C?

Every bank and credit-granting institution has a supply of historical data available: the records of their past customers, including those customers' characteristics. All that is needed is a tool to (1) evaluate the relative importance of the characteristics, and (2) apply the results to evaluating future customers. That tool, of course, is regression.

One of the largest savings and loan associations did just that: tabulated the characteristics of its past loan applicants, noted which applicants turned out to be good risks and which did not, isolated the most significant predictive characteristics by regression, and developed an equation to be used on new applications. The equation gave various weights to answers on the applicant's questionnaire, and resulted in a single number which could be used in ranking that applicant with others or in comparison with an arbitrary cutoff point below which applicants were considered bad risks.

But the organization did not stop there. They went on to test the equation on a large sample of new applications, and at the same time had the applications screened in the normal way by their loan officers. All the loans were granted and then watched carefully. The result was favorable to the mathematical approach: The regression equation not only gave fewer loans to people who did not in fact repay them, it also refused fewer loans to people who in fact paid promptly.

While financial institutions are among the most conservative organizations in existence, and loan officers in particular may resist lest their honor be smirched by a machine, more and more credit-grantors are considering or even using formulas like this. On a large scale this requires a great deal of computer time, but banks often have this at their disposal anyway, and once the original formula is worked out by computer a simplified but still accurate version can often be developed for hand use. If care is used, the computer may soon be supplying not only speed and accuracy but even increased justice in an emotion-fraught field.

Regression and Extrapolation Compared

Regression can also be used effectively in forecasting sales, as Parker and Segura have reported.* Their article presents an interesting comparison between regression and extrapolated trend lines as forecasting tools for construction industry product sales.

The regression formula used variables like purchasing power of customers and number of building permits issued. The trend lines were derived by fitting a least-squares line to the sales figures of the five most recent years and extrapolating. When the forecasts resulting from each method were compared, the regression method proved, not surprisingly, more accurate. The trend-line forecasts could very probably have been improved by using devices we shall discuss in the chapter on trends, but regression using appropriate variables would most likely still be better, because regression can take more information into account.

The key phrase above, of course, is *appropriate* variables: There are many situations in which it is by no means apparent what factors are relevant. And sometimes the relevant factors turn out to be the ones you are already using. For instance, what pieces of information would be most useful in predicting the number of pairs of shoes sold in your state next week? You might knock yourself out doing demographic studies and other research and then find that the most useful figures were those for sales last week and sales the same week a year ago—in other words, the same sales data you already use to project trend lines. In this case, the kind of analysis that proved ineffective in the building-products study would be more effective than regression. So trend lines and other time series forecasting methods also have their uses; they are discussed in the next major section.

---

* Parker and Segura, "How to Get a Better Forecast," *Harvard Business Review*, March–April 1971, pp. 99–109.

PART 3 | TIME SERIES FORECASTING

CHAPTER 4

EXPONENTIAL SMOOTHING

This chapter presents one of the most widely-known and useful notions in modern forecasting, a sophisticated sort of averaging called exponential smoothing. The name sounds formidable, but the mathematical concepts involved are usually introduced by the second year of high school, and this chapter should be fully understandable to a reasonably bright fifteen-year-old. The concepts are central to effective forecasting, however, especially with computers. They should therefore be understood thoroughly before you go on to later chapters.

THE BASIC IDEA

"Smoothing" here means averaging together; "exponential" refers to some mathematical formulas which turn up later. The simplest way to grasp what the two words mean together is to observe that one always has *some* forecast in mind, even if it is only a vague guess or expectation. For example, a manufacturer must forecast his future sales in order to plan production. He may do this by any method, including "seat-of-the-pants" or "feel-for-the-industry" guesses, and he may not even call the result a forecast, but that is what it is.

If he does this routinely at the end of each month, then before making a new forecast he can reflect on the accuracy of the forecast he made for the month just ended. Sales may have turned out to be 100 units higher than the forecast, for instance. This would suggest that the forecast for the next month should be increased, because this month's experience shows that the forecast used previously was too low.

But should the new forecast be increased by the full 100 units? That is, if the forecast made for this month's sales was 500, and actual sales were 600, should next month's forecast be 600? Probably not, because some of the extra sales may have been due to random fluctuations in the sales level. On the other hand, some of the error may have been due to actual increases in demand, or to actual deficiencies in the forecast.

Logically, then, we should increase the forecast by some part of the error observed, some fraction of the difference between the forecast and the actual value. In mathematical symbols, where F(T) was the forecast for this month and F(T + 1) represents the forecast for next month, the revising procedure can be stated as follows:

$$F(T + 1) = F(T) + \text{(fraction of error)}.$$

This is the procedure called exponential smoothing. The fraction used is usually about one-tenth, or 0.10 in the decimal form that computers require. In the example above, with that value the forecast becomes

$$F(T + 1) = 500 + \text{(fraction}*100)$$

$$= 500 + (0.10*100)$$

$$= 500 + 10$$

$$= 510.$$

If the error is negative, the same procedure is followed. Suppose in month T + 1 sales are actually 450 instead of the forecast 510. The forecast for month T + 2 then becomes

$$F(T + 2) = F(T + 1) + \text{(fraction}*\text{error)}.$$

The error in this case is the actual 450 minus the forecast 510, and is, therefore, negative; 450 minus 510 equals minus-60. So

$$F(T + 2) = 510 + (0.10*(-60))$$

$$= 510 + (-6)$$

$$= 510 - 6$$

$$= 504.$$

In brief, one way of looking at exponential smoothing is as a procedure for continually revising an expected value in the light of more recent experiences. The forecast is revised upward if the more recent value is higher than the forecast; it is revised downward if experience shows a lower actual value than was forecast. The amount by which the forecast is increased or decreased is proportional to the error.

Examples

One of the best ways to exhibit forecasting data, especially simple time series such as monthly sales, is to graph them. The first few figures in this chapter show the results of applying the simple exponential smoothing procedure to some actual data on the usage of various parts and supplies in a large industrial operation, in this case mining.

The graphs show a number of things clearly. First, the line which connects the dots indicating smoothed values is in fact a great deal smoother than the raw data. The term *smoothing* is an accurate metaphor. Second, some of the graphs show distinct trends in the data. For instance, the monthly usages of ammonium powder shown in Fig. 4.1 are gradually increasing. The effect of this increase is that the forecast, even after correction, is usually a bit low. As a result, the smoothed values don't reflect the actual process accurately enough. The problem of trends is dealt with in the next chapter, but the figure is a good example of the general problem of insufficient or inaccurate models. Figure 4.2 shows other examples of exponential smoothing.

The smoothing factor is the proportion or fraction of the error used as a correction, and is denoted H in this book. (It is sometimes called β, the Greek character beta.) As we noted above, it is usually 0.10 or near that value, and the graphs here show why. Smaller values produce smoother models but less responsive ones, while higher values are often too reflective of random "noise" in the data.

Simple statistical procedures for determining the best smoothing constants have been worked out, and these can be important where several factors in a model, such as the levels and trends discussed in the next chapter, must be smoothed simultaneously. But in most cases these procedures work no better than just graphing some trial constants and inspecting the graphs for a suitable mixture of smoothness and responsiveness.

Exercise 1. You manufacture tractors. The government of Ruritania has received a billion-dollar grant from the United Nations to convert from cut-and-slash nomadic farming to modern methods, and your company receives the order. Your sales for that month are equal to your firm's entire income for the past six years. Should the sales for the month the order is received be used in updating the sales forecast?

Exercise 2. You work for an aggressive company whose sales have been increasing at a rate of about 10% per month. Is the exponential forecasting procedure described above the one for you? Why or why not? If you're not sure, try working out an example and graph the results.

Exercise 3. You are a successful but vain television comedian. You have hired a statistician to forecast the size of the audience for your weekly show.

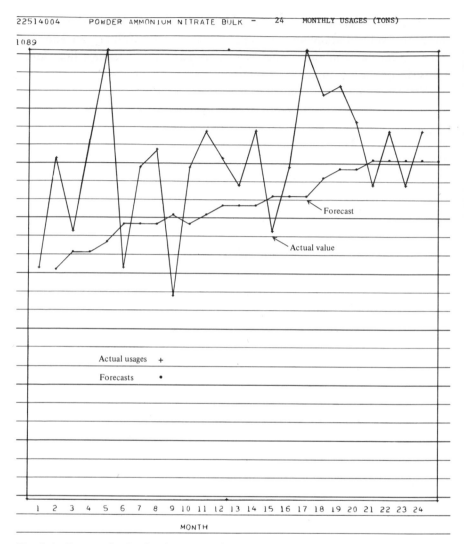

Fig. 4–1 Forecasting by simple exponential smoothing. The forecast shown is the result of applying the simple smoothing procedure to past actual data. Note how an unusually large usage is followed by an increased forecast for the next month, and the reverse for unusually low usages, as the forecast "learns" from experience.

One week your show occurs on Christmas Day and the audience is double its usual size. The statistician applies his standard exponential smoothing program to produce the next forecast. Should you object? What will you say?

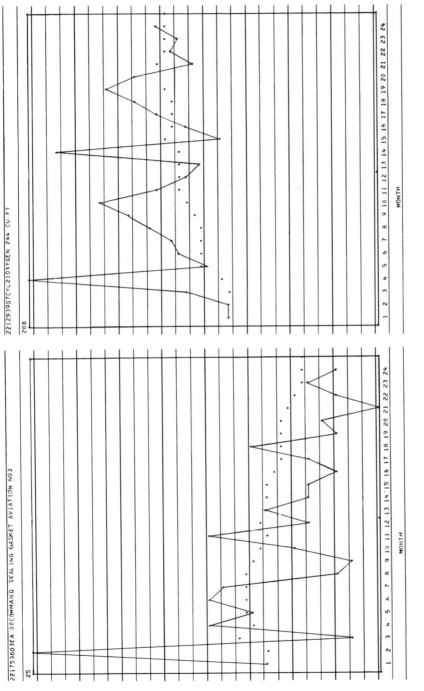

Fig. 4–2 Further examples of exponential smoothing.

Exercise 4. You manufacture three styles of psychedelic headbands. You think that sales of the leather one are increasing while the beaded and macramé styles seem to be selling less, but the figures for all three fluctuate violently from month to month as you market in new areas. Can you use exponential smoothing? What information can correlation give you?

How Does Updating Help?

Implicit in the simple exponential smoothing procedure described above is the basic notion of updating a guess or estimate on the basis of experience. As experience accumulates, one's estimates can be improved, and this procedure gives you an easy, consistent, numerical way of doing the improving. Smoothing is an absurdly simple procedure, but it is not trivial or foolish; it is, in fact, a very powerful and useful instrument.

Estimates need to be updated because the thing estimated may be changing. A company's sales may be increasing or decreasing; a comedian's audience may be growing or shrinking. An estimate made five years ago of the number of cars on the road will almost certainly not apply to today's traffic. Even death rates and tax percentages change, so you can be fairly certain that your forecasts are going to need updating to take care of new facts. Since they'll need it eventually, you might as well get maximum benefit from the procedure by doing it routinely and with reasonable frequency, especially if a computer is available and the new data can be gathered automatically as by-products of normal sales and accounting processing. This is one of the ideas behind most management information systems (MIS), but that is a subject for another book.

Exponential smoothing is especially useful because it can be applied to many things. These may be fields as diverse as a comedian's audience and a tractor manufacturer's sales. More important, they may be different factors within the same model. For instance, if sales or audiences are increasing, they must be going up at some average rate. What is it? You can make an estimate based on recent history, or just take a wild guess, and then update it as experience accumulates. This is the basis of trend forecasting, discussed in the next chapter. Similarly, if the beach umbrellas or antifreeze you manufacture sell more in one season than in another, you need to estimate the importance of the seasonal factor. Seasonality is again the topic of a later chapter, but you can guess right now that exponential smoothing is a major technique for improving your estimates of its influence.

In other words, exponential smoothing can be applied to any factor incorporated in a forecasting model. A forecasting situation, as we noted in

Chapter 1, is generally thought of as an underlying process with recognized components, together with a random "noise" element. The model you use to describe this underlying process may incorporate trends, seasonal factors, promotional expenditures, competitors' activities, technological progress or obsolescence, and many other factors. In any such model there are numerical values, or parameters, to be estimated. These estimates change the model from a theoretical framework to a useful and realistic tool. And exponential smoothing is an extremely useful method of estimating those parameters.

These comments are not intended to indicate that exponential smoothing is the only useful method for forecasting. In point of fact, methods like regression and correlation, which rely on understanding the relation of the factor being predicted to other, measurable, factors, can often be equally important. Nevertheless, in simple time series forecasting or in more complex models, exponential smoothing is one of the building blocks most often encountered and most likely to be of use.

Simple smoothing, as described above, is obviously easy to use. That is one argument in favor of using it. However, there are some apparent arguments against using it. For instance, it does not take into account any of the concurrent events which affect organizations and influence sales and other factors. It does not contain any structure that enables it to respond to advertising campaigns or product promotions in business. In the public sector, smoothing might be used to forecast public school populations; but while administrators may know about the closing of a local parochial school and its probable effect, there is no way to incorporate this factor in the simple smoothing model.

For reasons like these, many business and government organizations use the services of human forecasters. These are people familiar with the field who are routinely given information on advertising, competition, market or product changes, and other factors. Their job is to use this information, together with any statistical information they wish, to forecast sales or any other figures their employers require. (Government services, of course, may be regarded as sales to a particular market.)

Is this a good idea? The question we should ask is not whether human forecasters take more information into account than simple smoothing can, because obviously they do, but whether their forecasts are in fact more accurate as a result. It is often difficult to focus attention on the question of ultimate accuracy because so much energy goes into market research and analysis, but the results of investigating the issue are worthwhile.

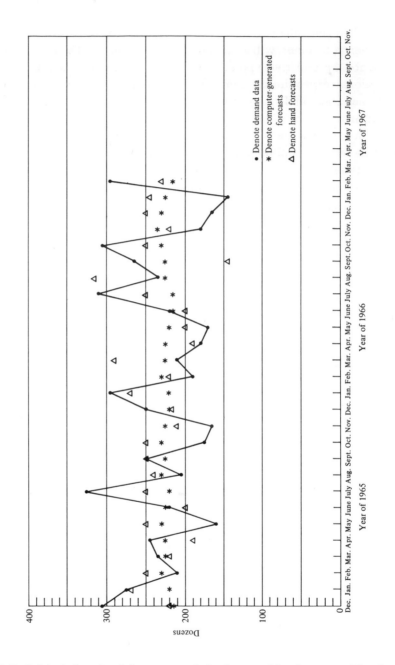

Fig. 4–3 Original data, hand forecasts, and simple smoothing forecasts. The simple smoothing is more accurate than the hand forecasts, which depend on judgment. From an unpublished study by Arthur D. Little, Inc., 1968.

Most often, the answer is that simple statistical forecasting is *more* accurate than forecasts made by market analysts or sales departments. Figure 4–3 shows a comparison of hand forecasts and computer-generated forecasts for a health-care product, one of many manufactured by a large pharmaceutical-supplies company. There is a good deal of variability in the actual sales, from about 150 to about 300 dozen per month in the years under consideration. The computer-generated forecasts, which result from simple exponential smoothing of actual past sales figures, are much less variable, and form a relatively smooth line through the more variable actual data. The hand-made forecasts also graphed in the exhibit are, in strong contrast, highly variable. They are, in fact, more variable than the actual data; the lowest hand forecast is lower than the lowest actual monthly sale, and the highest is higher than all but one of the actual sales figures. Some simple arithmetic applied to the two forecasts shows that the smoothing procedure is, in fact, somewhat more accurate than the hand forecasts.

Why should hand-generated forecasts made by experienced market professionals, in possession of complete information on both the market and promotional activities, be less accurate than an insensitive statistical technique? The answer seems to lie in the high variability of the manual forecasts. Human forecasters seem to overreact to factors like competitive actions and promotional activities, to think that they will have more effect than they actually do. A good deal of discussion of this effect has taken place in management circles over the past few decades, and most experienced forecasters agree that it has an emotional basis. Marketing departments are usually responsible for sales forecasting, and sales targets are so important to them that they exaggerate their expectations of their own sales promotions and, on the other hand, overemphasize the effects of competitors' actions. The same effect no doubt applies to school and church administrators, government service agencies, charity organizers, and anyone who makes forecasts for his own use.

In the end, then, exponential smoothing alone is often more accurate than forecasts made by people who are associated with the outcome. This does not mean that there is no value in human forecasts, but only that they must be tempered with some sort of statistical analysis. This subject and others concerning the management of forecasting will be discussed further in the final chapter.

OTHER KINDS OF AVERAGING

Exponential smoothing is actually a kind of averaging, a method of canceling out present excesses with data from the past. The theme of the next few sections is that the other common kinds of statistical averaging, moving and weighted averages, are very closely related to exponential smoothing. In fact, if the moving average approach is used in connection with an estimate of the oldest data point in the average, the result turns out to be identical with exponential smoothing. And weighted averages are the same even without any special assumptions, as long as you combine weighted averages of new data with the previous average.

Moving Averages

Knowing that averaging can help you to deal with fluctuating present values, you might wonder what would happen if you simply averaged *all* the available past data. The difficulty with this approach is that it gives the same importance to both the first and last data points. In real life, conditions usually change gradually over time, so that the oldest data are not as significant as the newest. One way to deal with this problem is simply to throw away the oldest data. If carried to its logical extreme, this would mean that the best estimator of the next value is the last one, and in some circumstances this is true. (Is this true of stock prices?)

However, there is usually enough random fluctuation in the data so that you must use more than simply the latest data point. The number of periods which should be used depends on the amount of random fluctuation in the data, and the rapidity with which the actual level is changing. A rapidly-changing level argues for a small number of values.

The number of data points used in constructing a moving average is generally denoted N; the moving average at a given time, denoted T, is then MN(T). The value of your factor at time T is X(T), and $X(T - N + 1)$ is the first value in your data series. The whole moving-average formula is then

$$MN(T) = \frac{X(T - N + 1) + X(T - N + 2) + \cdots + X(T)}{N}.$$

Presented in this way, the formula looks impressively technical, but a little thought and perhaps a few tries with sample numbers should grant you a revelation. The formula might just as well be

$$AVG = \frac{A + B + C + \cdots + X}{N},$$

where A, B, C, and so on are your values and N is the number of them you have. In fact, it is precisely the averaging formula you learned in grade school.

Why, then, bother with the long way around? Mostly because That's The Way It's Done: the way it appears in statistics texts, the way your statisticians are likely to present it, the way it might turn up on computer printout. You'll probably be seeing it in this form, and if you know what the letters mean you'll be better prepared to cope with the concepts involved. Second, and somewhat less important, using symbolism based on time reminds you of the basic difference between a simple average and a moving one. You take an ordinary average once, for all time; a moving average is calculated again and again, adding a new value at each time period and dropping an old one. If the present is always time T, the formula above serves as a reminder that each of the values must be moved.

Exercise 1. The numbers 7, 6, 6, 9, 7, 8, 4, 8, 7 are part of a random distribution centered around a specific value. Calculate moving averages for this series with $N = 3$ and $N = 6$; graph the averages for periods $T = 7$ through $T = 10$. What is the difference between the average error for M3 (the moving average when $N = 3$) and that for M6?

Exercise 2. Suppose a process is represented by a trend model; that is, the values are taken from a random distribution around a line which increases by a given amount each period, for example, the series 3, 4, 5, 6 . . . . What kind of error does M3 have? What about M6?

Exercise 3. Convert M3(3) (the average for the third period, using three data points) into M3(4) for the series 1, 2, 3, 4.

Updating a moving average, as in the last exercise above, is as simple in practice as in the example. You maintain a file of the last N data points, N being the number you want to use in the average. Then when a new value is received you subtract the first (oldest or earliest) value and add the new one. A clerk with a ledger can do it, but where many items are involved a computer is obviously more efficient. Then you recalculate the average; using the same symbolism as in the original equation, the new formula is

$$MN(T + 1) = \frac{MN(T) - X(T - N + 1) + X(T + 1)}{N}.$$

Relation to Exponential Smoothing

The discussion of exponential smoothing presented earlier in the Basic Idea section was really a plausibility argument. It was in no sense a mathematical proof that the procedure does anything specific or is in any sense accurate.

However, there is a good deal of appeal in the notion of correcting an estimate in accordance with errors as knowledge of those errors accumulates. That is what a mathematician would call an intuitive argument; there are also other intuitive arguments for the utility of exponential smoothing, somewhat more mathematical than the first. One of these is presented later, at the end of Chapter 6. We can look at another one right now.

Suppose you have been employing a moving average with $N = 4$ to forecast sales of the motorized Japanese tricycles you distribute. The clerk who calculates the average maintains his records on a long scroll of paper; the man is an inveterate smoker and one day the beginning of the scroll catches fire. Before he puts it out, the scroll is destroyed down to $T - 3$. Thereafter, $X(T - 2)$ is the first number available for calculating the moving average forecast $F(T)$. The formula for your next forecast, $F(T + 1)$, is $(X(T) + X(T - 1) + X(T - 2) + X(T - 3))/4$. In order to go on using the same sort of average, then, you will have to find some substitute for the actual value $X(T - 3)$ which is no longer available. One way to estimate any value, as we have noted before, is simply to average the available data. In this case, you already have the average of the last four observed values; that is exactly what $F(T)$, your last forecast, is.

You can therefore replace the lost value $X(T - 3)$ with $F(T)$ and use the formula for updating the moving average to derive a simpler formula. The updating formula is

$$F(T + 1) = F(T) - (X(T - 3)/4) + (X(T)/4), \qquad \text{or}$$

$$F(T + 1) = F(T) + (X(T) - X(T - 3)/4).$$

Replacing the lost value $X(T - 3)$ by the estimate $F(T)$ gives you

$$F(T + 1) = F(T) + (X(T) - F(T))/4.$$

$X(T) - F(T)$ is, of course, simply the forecast error at time T. In other words, the formula we have derived is simply that of exponential smoothing with H, the smoothing factor, set to one-fourth. Using any other number of data points in your moving average would give the same result but with a different smoothing factor.

Exercise 1. Repeat the derivation above for $N = 6$. What H-value do you get? For any given N, what is the corresponding value of H?

Exercise 2. Do you think that smoothing or the moving average should in general be more accurate? That is, should the average error be larger or smaller when a smoothing approach is taken than when a moving average is used? Is the average error an appropriate measure of accuracy?

Exercise 3. One of the advantages of exponential smoothing as opposed to the moving average approach is that records of past observations need not be maintained. The only information about the past which is needed is the current value of the current smoothed value, F(T). Is this an advantage? Is it a significant advantage? Is it a disadvantage? Does it make any difference?

Weighted Averages

The moving average does take care of the problem of old and perhaps less relevant data. It does so simply by getting rid of it, by dropping it from the computation. But the data remaining are all counted equally. Does this reflect reality? Perhaps older data should be counted less heavily than newer information, even after you have discarded the very oldest. Or maybe you shouldn't discard the oldest at all, but should include it as a small-significance factor.

This line of thought leads to an alternative averaging method called the weighted average. It is just as effective as the moving average, and somewhat easier to use. Whilst the data-shifting steps required to update a moving average can be confusing and easily fouled up, the weighted average updating procedure is straightforward and simple.

The basic idea of giving more weight or significance to recent data is applied by using a formula suggested by ordinary arithmetic averaging. The common formula for an arithmetic average of two values, X1 and X2, is $(X1 + X2)/2$. In other words, you take the sum of the values and divide by the number of data points.

You can also look at this somewhat differently. $(X1 + X2)/2$ is the same as $(X1)/2 + (X2)/2$, and that is just another way of writing $\frac{1}{2}(X1) + \frac{1}{2}(X2)$. In other words, you can view averaging as a process of adding fractions of the various data points. Usually you take the same fraction of each data value, but this need not be so. You could, for instance, take one-third of X1 and two-thirds of X2. In this way you would be giving more weight to the second value than to the first.

Exercise. Suppose X1 = 5 and X2 = 9. Find the arithmetic average, $A = \frac{1}{2}(X1) + \frac{1}{2}(X2)$, and the weighted average, $W = \frac{1}{3}(X1) + \frac{2}{3}(X2)$. Then try other values for the weights. Would $\frac{1}{4}$ and $\frac{1}{8}$ work well? What happens if the sum of the weights is larger than one? Smaller?

Relation to Exponential Smoothing

The answer to the last question in the exercise shows that the sum of the weights must always equal one. Denoting the two weights W1 and W2, W1 + W2 = 1.0, or, turning it around a little, W1 = 1 − W2. We can therefore rewrite the weighted average formula as follows:

$$\text{Weighted average} = W1(X1) + W2(X2)$$

$$= (1 - W2)(X1) + W2(X2)$$

$$= X1 - (W2)(X1) + W2(X2)$$

$$= X1 + (W2)(X2 - X1).$$

And that last line is exactly the formula for exponential smoothing with H equal to W2, if you regard X1 as an initial estimate of the central value.

Any number of data points and combination of weights may be used, as long as the sum of the weights equals one. We can see the relationship more clearly by multiplying out the process of applying exponential smoothing to the sequence of values X1, X2, X3, . . . , XN. At each step the new forecast value F is found by adding H times the new data value to 1 − H times the old F-value:

$$F2 = H(X2) + (1 - H)(F1).$$

For instance, when we obtain the actual value X3 we get the next forecast, F3, by

$$F3 = H(X3) + (1 - H)(F2)$$

$$= H(X3) + (1 - H)(H(X2) + (1 - H)(F1)).$$

We can use X1 in place of F1, since it was the only value available at time 1. Making this substitution gives

$$F3 = H(X3) + (1 - H)(H(X2) + (1 - H)(X1))$$

$$= H(X3) + H(1 - H)(X2) + (1 - H)^2(X1).$$

At time 4 we get

$$F4 = H(X4) + (1 - H)(F3)$$

$$= H(X4) + H(1 - H)(X3) + H(1 - H)^2(X2) + (1 - H)^3(X1).$$

At each step, all the powers of (1 − H) increase by one, since the previous term is always multiplied by (1 − H). After N steps, the result is

$$FN = H(XN) + H(1 - H)(X(N - 1)) + H(1 - H)^2(X(N - 2))$$
$$+ H(1 - H)^3(X(N - 3)) + \cdots + (1 - H)^{N-1}(X1).$$

This is a kind of weighted average in which the weights are modified powers of $(1 - H)$. Since $(1 - H)$ is less than one, older data are given progressively less weight, in almost geometrical sequence. In a pure geometrical sequence, each weight is the same fraction of the previous one. Here, each weight is $(1 - H)$ times the previous one, except for the one associated with X1. The modification is necessary so that the sum of the weights equals one. For example, suppose H equals 0.1. Then $1 - H = 0.9$, and the first few weights are

$$W1 = H = 0.1,$$

$$W2 = H(1 - H) = 0.1*0.9 = 0.09,$$

$$W3 = H(1 - H)^2 = 0.1*0.9^2 = 0.081,$$

$$W4 = H(1 - H)^3 = 0.1*0.9^3 = 0.0729.$$

This suggests that the latest data point contributes 10% to the forecast, the previous one 9%, the one before that only 8.1%, and so on. Altogether, the last four data points account for about 34% of the forecast.

Exercise. In Chapter 3 we noted briefly that relationships described by regressions often change slowly over time. This change could eventually call for a new regression model, but less drastic methods might provide more continuity and better overall forecasts. Can the exponential smoothing approach to updating be used to update regression relationships? Try to make up a simple formula for updating the coefficients A and B, relating one independent variable and one dependent variable in a simple regression equation. Then try to do the same for a regression model with two independent variables, like $X = A + B1*V1 + B2*V2$.

A Pictorial View of Forecast Accuracy

The introductory chapter emphasized that understanding of forecast errors is integral to all forecasting work. With point values like the ones considered in this chapter, the meaning of "forecast error" is obvious: If X is the actual value observed and F is the forecast value, the error is simply $X - F$. We will see later that there are a variety of ways to summarize a series of forecast errors. One of the most useful is the average of the absolute values of the errors, which is called the Mean Absolute Deviation or MAD. (Question:

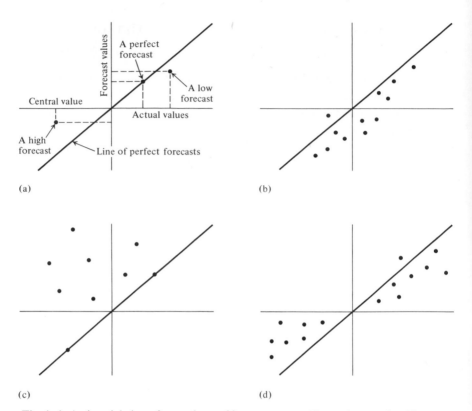

(a)   (b)

(c)   (d)

Fig. 4–4 A pictorial view of several sets of forecast errors. These pictures should suggest the proper remedial action. For example, how could you improve the accuracy of the system reflected in (d), which underestimates variability; in (b), which underestimates; and in (c), which overestimates?

Can you replace the average with a smoothed absolute error? Does this alternative have any advantages?) The MAD and other statistical measures are discussed at length in Chapter 7. But there is also a pictorial alternative, shown in Fig. 4–4.

This method is based on a Cartesian graph, in which the horizontal coordinate of each point is the actual value of a factor, and the vertical coordinate is the forecast value. The figure shows several hypothetical graphs and suggests interpretations of the patterns. A simple computer program can generate similar graphs for your forecasts, providing a fast and easy way to analyze the kinds of errors that occur as well as their magnitude. Later chapters will present several variations on this pictorial approach, each visualizing different aspects of error.

CHAPTER 5

TRENDS

The simple exponential smoothing approach described in the last chapter is an efficient and responsive way of estimating the actual level of some factor, such as sales or prices, when the factor can be conceived of as some steady central value which is affected by random fluctuations. The simple exponential smoothing technique is also appropriate when there are mild, gradual changes in the level of the factor.

However, when there is a strong upward or downward trend, the simple exponential smoothing technique will automatically introduce an error. This error can be serious. Therefore techniques have been developed for identifying trends and for estimating them when they exist. Just as in the case of simple exponential smoothing, the idea of making an estimate and then updating it as new information becomes available can be applied effectively to measuring trends. The statistics of this approach work out to a twofold formula in which both the level and the trend are stated explicitly and are updated when new information becomes available.

The result is a simple, understandable, and generally very satisfactory system for viewing trends. In the experience of industrial concerns over many years, the performance of level and trend forecasting systems has been more accurate than exponential smoothing of the level for factors like sales and inventory. Therefore, the additional effort of using trends is worthwhile from a practical point of view, which is not always the case with other possible refinements in forecasting systems.

WHAT HAPPENS IF THERE IS A TREND?

Consider monthly demands for an inventory item. That demand is generally subject to some random fluctuation; it may also be subject to a long-term growth or decline, depending on whether the product is new and gaining acceptance, or old and being phased out. Suppose, for the sake of illustration, that a hypothetical product has no random fluctuation in its demand, but that it is increasing at a steady rate, like the graph shown in Fig. 5–1.

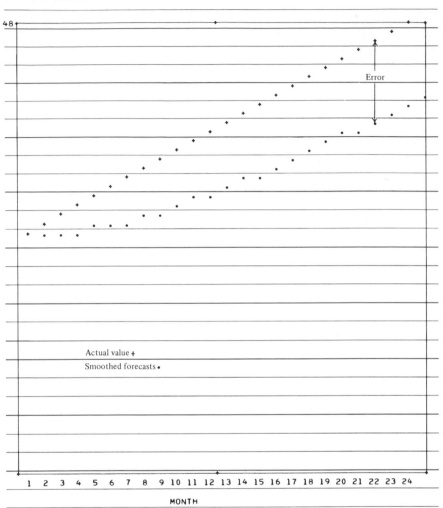

Fig. 5–1 Forecasting by simple exponential smoothing applied to a hypothetical upward-trending value. Note that the error introduced by this method increases up to a stable error level.

If the simple exponential smoothing approach to estimating the next monthly value is used, beginning with an estimate equal to the first month's sale, the smoothed value will lag behind the actual value. This is because the smoothed value is increased by only some percentage, usually a relatively low one, of the forecast error. For instance, if sales increase from 25 in the first month to 26 in the second month, and the forecast was 25, the error is

1.0, and the new forecast will only be 25 + (0.1∗1.0) = 25.1 if the smoothing constant is the standard ten percent.

In the third month, if sales are 27 units, the error will be 27 minus 25.1, or 1.9; this error is much larger than the previous one. It will produce a correspondingly larger correction, but not yet enough to make up the difference. The result is that the smoothed value drops below the actual value and stays there, as shown in Fig. 5–1. In other words, a permanent error is introduced by the use of the simple smoothing technique where there is a trend.

However, the error does not continue to increase forever. At some point, the error is so large that the correction factor becomes equal to the monthly increase. The correction factor, after all, is simply a fraction of the error; when this fraction is equal to the monthly increase, the smoothed line will increase at the same rate as the actual line. It will, of course be far below the actual line. (We are assuming, of course, a steady, unitary increase, adding the same number of units every month. If the increase is itself a fraction of the base figure, things get more complicated. The amount of the increase then increases every time. With this kind of increase, called exponential, the correction factor cannot catch up.)

Figure 5–2 presents an example of a real inventory item with declining demand. It comes from a study of the industrial operations of a major U.S. company. Simple exponential smoothing with H equal to 0.1 produces the curve shown. Obviously the curve is inappropriate, although it does pass through some of the data.

It is easy to show that the simple trend/error relationship stabilizes. Suppose that the smoothing constant in use is 0.1. Then the correction is equal to 0.1 times the forecast error. If the monthly increase is 50 units, the correction factor will equal the increase when the following equation holds:

$$0.1 * error = 50, \quad or \quad forecast \ error = 50/0.1 = 500.$$

This equation can be generalized for other updating factors besides 0.1. The error introduced by the inappropriate use of simple smoothing is equal to T/H, where T is the trend or monthly increase and H is the smoothing constant. For instance, if H had been 0.05 in the example above, instead of 0.1, the eventual stable error would have been 50/0.05, or 1000, rather than 500.

It is possible to deal with this constant error by simply adding it back in; that is, by adding T/H to the simple smoothed value. But avoiding the error altogether is better than coping with it. The next section describes a more appropriate model for trending values.

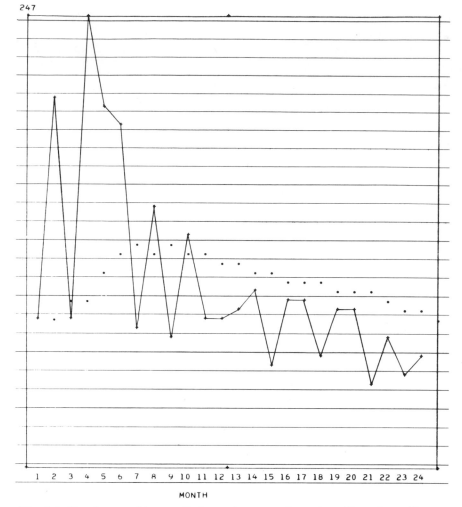

247

MONTH

Fig. 5–2 Simple smoothing applied to a down-trending value. Note the stable error resulting from the trend.

THE BASIC IDEA: UPDATING LEVEL AND TREND

A simple, straightforward, and useful method of dealing with trends consists of a two-stage procedure:

1. Begin with an estimate of the present level and the rate of increase or decrease, based on either judgment or past data.

2. Every time new data become available, or at convenient intervals,

update the estimates of both level and trend in proportion to the error in the latest forecast.

The difference between two successive values can be viewed as a very short-term data trend. The overall, long-term trend is the average of all these differences between two points, and each two-point difference can be regarded as an estimate of the long-term trend T. The two-point differences, then, play the same role in estimating the actual value of the long-term trend T as the data values play in estimating the level. Each time a new data point becomes available, a new two-point difference can be calculated and used to smooth the existing estimate of the trend. The new trend estimate T2 can be found by using the old trend estimate T1, the difference between the two most recent data values $X(T)$ and $X(T - 1)$, and the smoothing constant H, as follows:

$$T2 = T1 + H*(\text{two-point difference minus } T1)$$
$$= T1 + H*(X(T) - X(T - 1) - T1).$$

For instance, consider the data graphed in Fig. 5–3. This might represent monthly sales of some new product, or demands for a spare part in an industrial operation. On the basis of the three data points available to date, there appears to be a strong positive trend. The trend line drawn through those three data points represents a preliminary estimate; the height of the line at time 3 is 27.5 units, and the slope is 4.0 units. (We defer discussion of calculating this initial estimate until a later section of this chapter.)

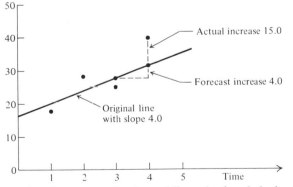

Fig. 5–3 Forecast based on extrapolated trend line. At time 3 the level of the line is 27.5 and the estimated trend (increase) is 4.0.

The forecast for time 4 can be made by simply extrapolating the straight line. The forecast is equal to the present level plus the estimated trend:

$$\text{Forecast} = \text{level} + \text{trend}$$

$$= 27.5 + 4.0$$

$$= 31.5.$$

Now, at the end of month 4, information becomes available on actual demand. As shown in Fig. 5–3, the next value was actually 40; the forecast was too low.

To correct this too-low forecast on our next try, we increase both the level and the trend by a small fraction of the error. This fraction might be the standard smoothing constant 0.1. That gives us the following formulas:

$$\text{New level} = \text{forecast level} + (0.1*\text{error in last forecast})$$

$$= 31.5 + (0.1*8.5)$$

$$= 32.35.$$

$$\text{New trend} = \text{old trend} + (0.1*\text{error in last trend})$$

$$= 4.0 + 0.1*(15.0 - 4.0)$$

$$= 4.0 + 1.1$$

$$= 5.1.$$

Note that the anticipated monthly increase was added in before updating the level. This avoids the problem produced by simple smoothing, in which the level is simply updated by a fraction of the error, without adding in the estimated trend. Also note that the error in the trend is calculated by regarding the trend as an estimate of the month-to-month increase. The increase from month 3 to month 4 is from 25 units to 40 units, or 15 units net. The estimate of 4.0 for the increase is obviously too small, and is adjusted upward using the smoothing factor. Updating the trend on the basis of the forecast error, rather than on this two-point difference, is incorrect and can lead to serious problems; this did happen in one forecasting system encountered by the author. (See discussion of "An Alternate Formula," later in this chapter.)

The net result of the updating steps above is a new estimate of the trend line. The new estimate is composed of a new present level, corresponding to time 4, and a new trend. The new trend line based on all four data points is shown in Fig. 5–4. Note that it has both a higher level and a higher slope than the line based on only the first three data points.

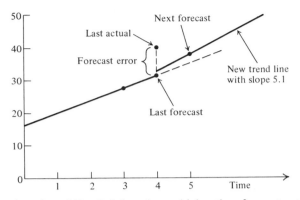

Fig. 5-4 Updated version of Fig. 5–3, based on a higher-than-forecast actual value at time 4. Note the higher level and the trend of the new line, and the new forecast based on it.

Exercise. Is it possible for an updated line to have a higher slope but a lower level than the previous line? Give an example.

The forecast for month 5 is easy to make on the basis of the new trend line:

$$\text{Forecast for T5} = \text{level as of T4} + \text{trend}$$

$$= 32.35 + 5.1$$

$$= 37.45.$$

Some typical sequences of forecasts for trending values are shown in Figs. 5–5 and 5–6. Only the forecasts for T + 1 made as of time T are shown; both level and trend are updated each month and fluctuate together.

Obviously, a good deal of arithmetic is involved in this procedure, and the trend model has only two variable factors. Doing this type of forecasting for a wide variety of products (if you are a wholesaler), for a large number of elementary schools (if you are a school district), or for a large number of stocks (if you are trying to get rich quick), is obviously easier with a computer.

A Note on Notation

Statements about forecasts are confusing and complicated to write down because there are two times involved: the time *at which* the forecast is made, and the time *for which* it is made. Sentences like "The month 3 sales forecast for month 10 was too high" are hard to sort out.

```
DJIA WEEKLY CLOSINGS BEGINNING 1 07 70
   802.0      787.0      782.0      759.0      754.0      757.0
   757.0      768.0      788.0      778.0      768.0      790.0
   792.0      790.0      776.0      747.0      734.0      717.0
   702.0      662.0      700.0      695.0      684.0      699.0
     0.0        0.0        0.0        0.0        0.0        0.0
     0.0        0.0        0.0        0.0        0.0        0.0
     0.0        0.0        0.0        0.0
```

```
AVERAGE        802
INITIAL LEVEL AND TREND                          802.00        0.00

SMOOTHING FACTORS FOR A1   A2   XMAD    .10    .05    .10
TRACKING SIGNAL THRESHOLD        .70
```

MO	ACT	XHAT	ERR	XMAD	SE	A1	A2	TRACK
2	787	802	-15	27	11	800	-.8	.42
3	782	800	-18	26	8	798	-1.6	.32
4	759	796	-37	27	4	793	-3.5	.14
5	754	789	-35	28	-0	786	-5.3	.00
6	757	780	-23	28	-2	778	-6.4	.09
7	757	772	-15	26	-4	770	-7.2	.14
8	768	763	5	24	-3	763	-6.9	.12
9	788	757	31	25	1	760	-5.3	.03
10	778	754	24	25	3	757	-4.1	.12
11	768	753	15	24	4	754	-3.4	.18
12	790	751	39	25	8	755	-1.4	.30
13	792	753	39	27	11	757	.5	.40
14	790	758	32	27	13	761	2.1	.48
15	776	763	13	26	13	764	2.8	.50
16	747	767	-20	25	10	765	1.8	.38
17	734	767	-33	26	5	764	.1	.21
18	717	764	-47	28	0	759	-2.2	.01
19	702	757	-55	31	-5	751	-4.9	.17
20	662	746	-84	36	-13	738	-9.2	.37
21	700	729	-29	35	-15	726	-10.6	.42
22	695	715	-20	34	-15	713	-11.6	.45
23	684	702	-18	32	-16	700	-12.5	.48
24	699	687	12	30	-13	689	-11.9	.43

```
FINAL LEVEL AND TREND                            688.57      -11.93

XMAD   SMOOTHED ABS ERROR              30.20

SMOOTHED ERROR                        -12.86
```

Fig. 5–5 An example of exponential smoothing with both a level and a trend. A1 is the level and A2 is the trend; the forecast for the next month is A1 + A2 and is denoted by XHAT. ACT indicates actual values; ERR is the error; XMAD, SE, and TRACK are measures of variability that will be discussed later.

The least confusing way around this difficulty is to assume that forecasts are always made at the latest time for which actual data are available; this is always called time T. Then the forecast for the next time period is the forecast for time T + 1, or in symbols F(T + 1) (as in Fig. 5–7). Then the most common terms which occur in forecasting can be denoted as follows:

DJIA WEEKLY CLOSINGS BEGINNING 1 07 70

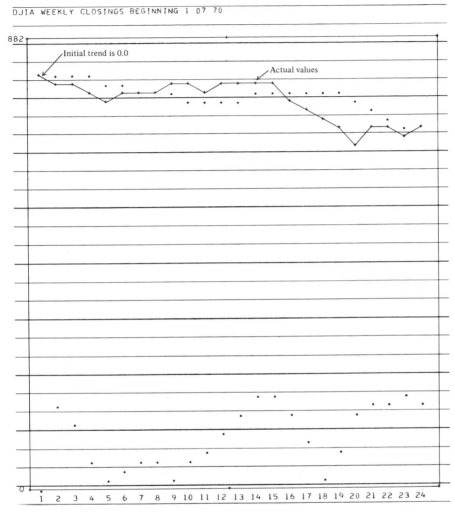

Fig. 5–6 Graph of the smoothed trend forecasts calculated in Fig. 5–5. (Tracking signal threshold = 0.7; no signals. Lower curve is [ABS(SE)/XMAD]∗.4∗882.)

A1(T) denotes the present level, including the latest updating.

A2(T) denotes the present estimate of the trend. T is not a good symbol for trend because it gets confused with T for time.

F(T + 1) denotes the forecast for the next time period.

F(T) indicates the forecast of the present value made in the previous

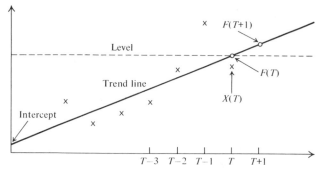

Fig. 5–7 Illustration of notation; the × indicate actual data points and the o are forecasts.

time period, T − 1. This forecast is updated at time T to produce the next forecast, F(T + 1).

X(T) is the actual observed value at time T.

ERR(T) denotes the most recent observed error, X(T) − F(T).

H1 denotes the updating constant for the level; H2 is the updating constant for the trend.

XHAT is often used to indicate the particular forecast under discussion. The term comes from the statistician's "hat" symbol for an estimate, X.

The forecast made for two time periods ahead is then F(T + 2), and so on. This type of notation is simpler to read in practice than alternatives like F(3, 4) which indicate explicitly both the present month and the month for which the forecast is being made. The only disadvantage is that the time at which the forecast is made is not included, but this rarely leads to confusion.

The significant thing to remember is that the word "level" always refers to the present level of the estimated trend line. In high school mathematics a trend line is described by giving its slope and its initial value. The initial value is called the intercept, because it intercepts the y-axis of the conventional graph at point zero. Computer programs often produce results noted in this form. While a conversion program must be used to turn these results into the form we are using here, it is a relatively easy step and worthwhile because this form is easier conceptually.

Exercise 1. On a piece of scratch paper, draw a straight line with a trend, either up or down. Draw an irregular, wavy line around the straight line, like the one shown in Fig. 5–8. Regard the horizontal scale as time and the vertical scale as the value of sales of your product. Find the sales for each month, 1 through 10, from the graph you have drawn.

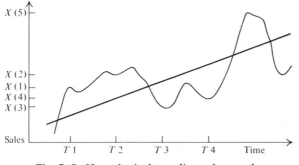

Fig. 5–8 Hypothetical trending sales graph.

Start with an estimate of the sales value equal to the first point you have chosen, and with an initial trend estimate of zero. Update the estimates for each of the nine following data points by using the method explained above. Use H1 and H2 equal to 0.1 and 0.05, or choose your own values. How does the result after nine periods compare with the actual trend and with the actual central or "model" value (which you know since you began with your own line)?

Then do it again, this time with a trend and level estimate equal to the actual value of the trend line as of time 1. Update for the next nine time periods using the same values you used above. How much error does the updating procedure introduce by comparison with the known line, after nine periods? What is the maximum error? At what time period does it occur? Does this surprise you?

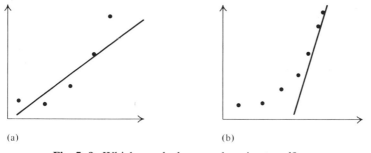

(a)   (b)

Fig. 5–9 Which graph shows a changing trend?

Exercise 2. Now perform the same set of exercises for data which do not lie on a trend line, but which instead show a changing trend. An example is sketched in Fig. 5–9. Would you expect your trend line to look more like (a) or (b) when you have finished with the updating process?

Exercise 3. In updating a trend line, should the trend be updated before the level? Does it matter? [*Hint*: Redraw Fig. 5–4 each way.]

Exercise 4. Will the average error increase or remain the same as forecasts are made for more distant periods—three months ahead, a year ahead, two years ahead, and so on?

Selecting Smoothing Constants

In general, a smaller smoothing constant should be used for updating the trend than for updating the level. This will result in a smoother series of forecasts, which is advantageous even if there is no difference in forecast error. One way of choosing a smoothing factor for the trend (H2) is to square the factor (H1) used for the level. If H1 is 0.1, then H2 will be 0.01. In the figures in this chapter, H1 equals 0.1 and H2 equals 0.05. Testing a variety of values for H1 and H2 in a given situation is usually the best approach, using a sample of historical data. The sample should cover the longest possible period.

An Alternate Formula

The method given above is not the most obvious one for updating an estimate of trend in a time series. In a university-level course which used a draft of this book as text, the students were asked to suggest a formula before reading the material on trends. The brightest student in the class, a chemistry PhD, was able to suggest a method and translate it into a formula precise enough for computer use. The formula turned out to be the same one presented in several technical publications on forecasting methods, including an IBM systems manual* and a textbook on management science by a leading forecasting expert, R. G. Brown.† All of these recommend that the trend estimate be updated by a formula like the following:

$$T2 = T1 + H*ERR.$$

In English, this would read, "The new trend is the result of correcting the old trend by adding a fraction of the error to it." For instance, if the forecast

---

* *Retail IMPACT*—Inventory Management and Control Techniques—Application Description Manual (GE20-0188).

† Brown, R. G., *Management Decisions for Production Operations,* Dryden Press, Hinsdale, Ill., 1971, p. 61.

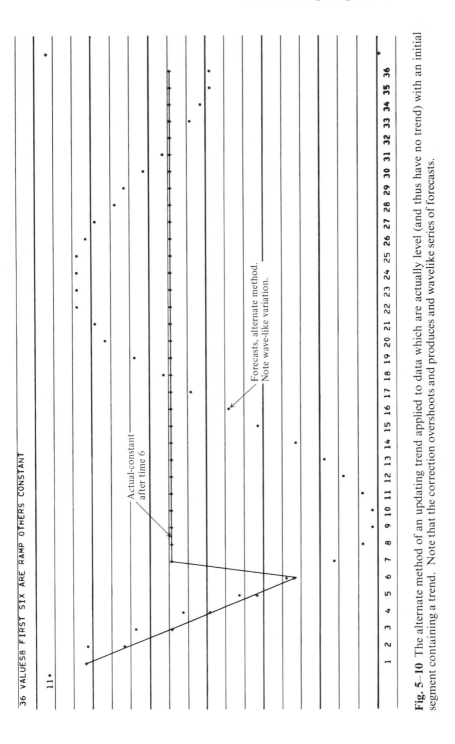

36 VALUES8 FIRST SIX ARE RAMP OTHERS CONSTANT

Actual-constant
after time 6

Forecasts, alternate method.
Note wave-like variation.

Fig. 5–10 The alternate method of an updating trend applied to data which are actually level (and thus have no trend) with an initial segment containing a trend. Note that the correction overshoots and produces and wavelike series of forecasts.

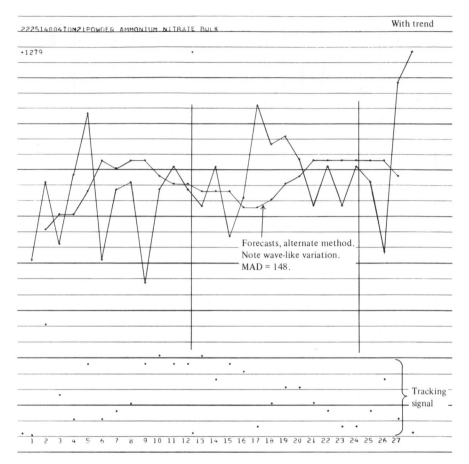

Fig. 5–11 Alternate trend updating method applies to some real nontrending data. The same wavelike forecast pattern turns up—inappropriately. MAD is a measure of forecast accuracy.

is 115 and the observed value is 135, the trend would be increased when the updating procedure is applied.

Exercise. Suppose a time series really has no trend, but that for some reason the estimate of the level is too low. Assume that the estimate of the trend is correct (namely, T2 = 0.0). What is the trend after updating? Is the trend after updating still correct? Suppose the data are almost unvarying. Will the forecast increase to the correct level? What will the trend be at that point? What will happen in the next several forecasts?

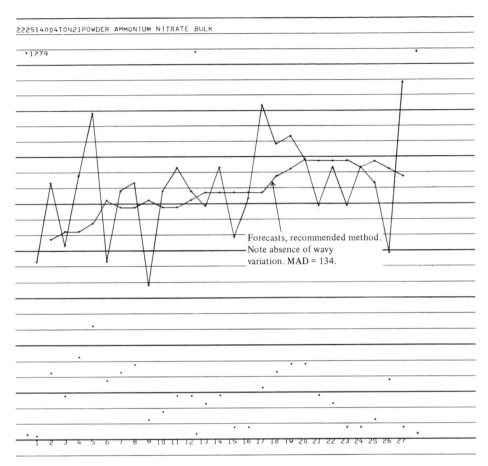

Fig. 5-12 The method introduced and recommended earlier, applied to the same data. Note the absence of wavelike patterns in the forecasts, and the lower MAD indicating greater accuracy with this method (for these data).

Figure 5–10 shows what happens if an incorrect level is assumed for data which actually have no trend, and updated by means of this approach. In this case, the initial level and trend are inappropriate because a down-trending pattern for the first six periods produces forecasts unrelated to the later data, which are constant. As shown, the trend in the forecasting procedure increases as long as the forecast is less than the actual data, even when it is quite close. When the forecast is equal to the actual level, the trend has built up to a substantial size—and the forecast overshoots the actual level. Then it corrects itself, only to reverse the process and overshoot on the way down.

The result is a wavelike series of forecasts. It does gradually settle down to the correct level; note that the error in the second loop is less than the error in the first, and that the error in the third is less than in the second. This corrective action is fairly rapid in the hypothetical example, where the level data really are level. Figure 5–11 shows the same calculations applied to real data with substantial variation. The same wavelike progress occurs, but here it is not so quickly damped out, because of the random variation in the data.

Both of these sets of forecasts were made by a commercially available forecasting program which used the formula given above. Figure 5–12 shows the result of using the forecasting method recommended in earlier parts of this chapter. It looks more appropriate, exhibits no wavelike variation, and produces a smaller average forecast error for these data. In fact, updating with no trend at all is more accurate than using the alternate formula.

The conclusion to be drawn is not clear. It would be too strong to say that the alternate formula is "wrong." Yet it clearly gives misleading results in some circumstances. Furthermore, the concept of estimating a trend by reference to an error based on level alone is not as appealing as the notion of estimating trends by means of a series of two-point trends. On the other hand, the argument can be made that in practical situations there is rarely enough information available to estimate trends without reference to level and forecast error. This argument is made by means of some fairly sophisticated mathematics in some well-known works on forecasting,* yet some experiences, like the ones displayed in the figures, suggest that it is sometimes inappropriate.

The most natural conclusion to draw is that thought and testing are needed in the design of a forecasting system. If more than one method is considered, a decision should be based on actual testing of the forecast accuracy, using samples of historical data. No forecasting method is really "wrong", but many are inappropriate for a given circumstance. Incidentally, the student who re-invented this method decided that he preferred the other one, once the difference had been pointed out.

INITIAL ESTIMATES OF TREND LINES

The updating procedures for improving the estimates of level and of trend are, by necessity, applicable only to previous estimates. They are means of improving estimates, not of creating them in the first place. As a result, a

---

* For example, Brown, R. G., *Smoothing, Forecasting, and Prediction of Discrete Time Series*, Prentice-Hall, Englewood Cliffs, N.J., 1962.

forecasting system which involves trends must be begun with an initializing phase in which the original estimates of level and trend are produced.

Generally, when you are installing a forecasting system in an ongoing enterprise some historical information is available. For instance, when a company decides to install a computerized inventory control system for its products, most of the products already exist. Sales information of some kind will probably be available for each product, often on a monthly or quarterly basis. There may even be some sort of forecasting system. This information can be used to provide initial estimates of the sales level and the trend, if any, for each of the items.

From a statistical point of view the problem of estimating the level and trend factors A1 and A2 on the basis of historical information is quite different from the problem of improving the estimates as additional information becomes available. Typically two different sets of computer programs are used. The first set, referred to as the *initializing* programs, is used only once when the system is set up. The *updating* routines are then used periodically to accomplish the improvements in estimates described in the first part of this chapter.

Nearly all the initializing programs for estimates of level and trend available today are based upon the idea of a *least-squares* fit, which is a way of finding the trend line through historical data in such a way that the line is the "best" one in the sense described below.

The Least-Squares Concept

Suppose that you are the planner for a computerized accounting service,

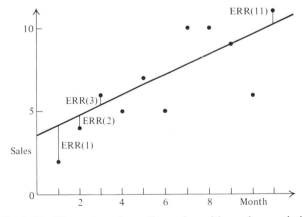

Fig. 5–13 Illustration of trending value with random variation.

and that the following figures represent the firm's monthly sales for the past year:

$$2, 4, 6, 5, 7, 5, 10, 10, 9, 6, 11, 13.$$

Graphing these data gives the picture shown in Fig. 5–13.

Obviously, there is a strong trend in sales. (Congratulations—it is upward.) A line like the straight line drawn on the graph can be considered a model of the growth in sales. At each time interval T, the model value (on the line) differs from the actual value by some amount, possibly zero, called the error or deviation, and denoted ERR(T) since there is a separate error for each time period.

Measuring the Fit

How inaccurate is the model of the process given by the line, taken as a whole? One way to answer the question is simply to add up all the errors: overall inaccuracy equals $ERR(1) + ERR(2) + \cdots + ERR(N)$. Of course, this formula is too simple, because it doesn't take into account the *number* of data points. The solution is simple: Take the *average* error. If there were a mathematical method which could be used to find the one line which had the smallest average error, that line would be the best estimate of the underlying model.

There is a minor technical difficulty with this, and it is a mathematical one. One calculates the error by the formula

$$ERR(T) = X(T) - F(T),$$

where X(T) indicates the actual value at the time T and F(T) indicates the value of the model at time T (that is, the value of the trend line). If the actual value is less than the model value, the formula gives a negative result. If the errors calculated in this way are added, the negative and positive errors cancel out, giving a near-zero total. Even large errors could add up to an apparent zero total inaccuracy.

One way to get around this problem is simply to discard positive and negative signs, and add up the remaining *absolute values* of the errors. An alternative is to *square all the errors*; that is, to multiply each error by itself. The result of squaring is always positive. Both approaches are used in forecasting, but using the squared errors has proven more convenient in fitting lines.

If you square the errors the negative values are eliminated, and the average of the squared errors can be used as a measure of the overall accuracy of the trend line. Fortunately, it turns out to be easy to find the particular trend line which has the smallest average squared error. The formulas are simple, and the approach used in deriving them, detailed below, can also be used in a variety of ways later on to produce even more useful formulas.

Least-Squares Derivation

We want to find the optimum values for the intercept (the level at time zero) and the trend; we can start by assigning them the symbols A and B, respectively. Then at time T the relevant point on the trend line will be $A + (T*B)$. If we represent the actual values by X1, X2, and so on, then for time periods 1, 2, ..., N the values of the model and of the error are as follows:

Time	Model	Error
1	$A + B$	$X1 - (A + B)$
2	$A + 2B$	$X2 - (A + 2B)$
3	$A + 3B$	$X3 - (A + 3B)$
.	.	.
.	.	.
.	.	.
N	$A + NB$	$XN - (A + NB)$

The errors are all of the form $XT - (A + TB)$; the squared errors are therefore of the form $(XT - (A + TB))^2$. The total squared error (TSE) is then the sum of $(XT - (A + TB))^2$, where T equals 1, 2, ..., N.

An application of the basic idea of differential calculus can then be applied to produce the following two equations:

$$(1)\ \text{SUM OF } 2*(XT - (A + TB))*(-1) = 0,$$

$$(2)\ \text{SUM OF } 2*(XT - (A + TB))*(-T) = 0.$$

These are a pair of simultaneous equations like those covered in high school algebra. We can solve them for A and B:

$$B = \text{SUM OF } T*X(T)/\text{SUM of T-SQUARED, WHERE}$$

$$T = 1, 2, \ldots, N,$$

$$A = \text{AVERAGE OF XT's} - B*\text{AVERAGE OF T's}.$$

It is handy to remember that the line passes through the point (T,X), where T is the average T-value and X is the average X-value.

Note that this formula still applies even if the values of T are not all used, or are unevenly spaced. In fact, it works for any group of number pairs. They may be denoted T and X(T), or Y(I) and X(I), or in any other manner, as long as the values are ordinary numbers.

Exercise 1. Use the formula to find A and B for the series 2, 4, 6, 5, 7, 5, 10, 10, 9, 6, 11.

Exercise 2. In algebra it is customary to describe a trend line by specifying its value when X equals zero, called the *y*-intercept, and its slope. In statistical forecasting the trend line is conventionally described by its value or level at a particular time, time T, and the word trend is substituted for the word slope. When a level is referred to in forecasting and no time is specified, it is assumed that the most recent time is meant. Let A represent the level rather than the intercept value in the outline above, and rewrite the formulas with this new notation. If you are familiar with calculus, find the formulas for the best A and B. Are they the same as in the algebraic formulation?

Exercise 3. Can this argument be applied to absolute (that is, nonsquared but signless) errors? Why or why not?

Exercise 4. Try to decide how much difference there is between any two of the following:

1. the trend line calculated by least-squares,
2. the trend line produced by updating an initial estimate of the level and trend,
3. the trend line produced by sketching a guess through a graph.

Exercise 5. Calculate the level and trend for the following data:

Month	Sales
1	100
2	200
3	400
4	300
5	300

What is the level at time 0? At time 5? What is the forecast for time 6?

Exercise 6. For the data sketched in Fig. 5–14, what is unsatisfactory about the trend-line fitting method described above? What steps could be taken to eliminate this inadequacy?

Fig. 5–14 Data for which a simple trend model is not appropriate.

GIVING MORE WEIGHT TO MORE IMPORTANT DATA

A reader who is experienced in forecasting would answer the questions in the last exercise by noting that a simple least-squares fit is not appropriate because the trend is changing. The slope, initially quite high, has decreased markedly, so that now a rather small trend value would be appropriate. The trend line fitted by the least-squares approach does not reflect this; it produces a trend which is about halfway between the lowest and the highest. This is obviously misleading; the immediate future we are concerned with is most likely to resemble the recent past, so we need an accurate representation of the current trend.

The solution to problems like this is to *weight* recent data more heavily than older data. There are two fairly obvious ways to do this:

1. Exponential smoothing of level and trend gives less weight to older data, since at each step the older data are all multiplied by a factor smaller than one, namely, $1 - H$.

2. The least-squares fitted line approach could be used together with some method of weighting the data according to age.

Either approach will produce a satisfactory resolution of the problem. In fact, under certain circumstances the results of either approach will be the same. But for a variety of practical reasons the first approach is more effective. We will discuss these reasons after a brief look at how the weighted least-squares idea might be put into practice. As usual, the important factors are neither statistical nor technical.

Our objective is to reproduce in outline the reasoning that produces the best A1 and A2, but with the addition of weighting factors for age. These weighting factors should be relatively large for the most recent data, and should fall off, giving less and less weight to successively older data. Any number W smaller than one can be used to produce a set of reasonable weights as follows:

Time	Weighted error
N	1
N − 1	W
N − 2	W^2
.	.
.	.
.	.
1	W^N

For W = 0.9, for instance, these weights are 1.0, 0.9, 0.81, and so on. But the weights can't be used by simply multiplying each data point by the relevant weight; that would just produce small numbers for the older data, and result in a too-large A2.

A closely-related idea, however, can be used. Instead of applying the weights to the data values, we can use them on the errors. That is, in fitting the trend line we can give successively less importance to the fluctuations of older data, so that the resulting line will be strongly influenced by its deviations from recent values but less strongly by older ones.

The forecast value at time T for a line with intercept A and slope B is A + TB, and the error is XT − (A + TB). Multiplying this error by the weights B^T gives the following error list:

Time	Weighted error
1	$(X1 - A - 1B)(W^N)$
2	$(X2 - A - 2B)(W^{N-1})$
3	$(X3 - A - 3B)(W^{N-2})$
.	.
.	.
.	.
N	$(XN - A - NB)(W)$

The total of the squared weighted errors is then

$$\text{TSWE} = \text{SUM OF } (XT - A - TB)(W^{N-T+1}).$$

The same elementary calculus formulas used earlier produce another set of simultaneous equations, which can be solved to give formulas for the best weighted slope and intercept. The arithmetic is a bit more complicated because of the W factors, but not much. The resulting formulas are

$$A2 = (\text{SUM OF } W(I)*T(I)^2)/(\text{SUM OF } W(I)*X(I)*T(I)^2)$$

$$A1 = (\text{SUM OF } W(I)*X(I))/(\text{SUM OF } W(I)),$$

where $I = 1, 2, \ldots, N$ and where $T(I)$ represents the original data shifted by adding an amount S, where S is given by

$$S = -(\text{SUM OF } W(I)*T(I)/(\text{SUM OF } W(I)).$$

The weight $T(I)$ could be any number; as indicated above it is usually W^I, so that successive weights are successive powers of an initial weighting factor.

Exercise. If you are familiar with calculus, carry out the derivation of these formulas. One way to solve the simultaneous equations is to shift all values by an amount which makes the second term in the first equation equal to zero. This term is automatically zero in the nonweighted case.

Simulation of Exponential Smoothing

We are still dealing with the problem of how to estimate reasonable values for A1 and A2 during the initializing phase of forecasting when we are working with historical data. The weighted least-squares approach just described is one possible way. It is very neat from an intellectual or mathematical point of view, and it involves much less calculation than other methods. This would be of great importance if computers did not exist. However, since they do exist, we can consider another approach, which may be more fruitful: simulation of exponential smoothing.

   Simulating exponential smoothing requires two steps:

1. Start with some estimate of A1 and A2.
2. Update these initial values by using the actual available data values X1, X2, and so on.

   The first advantage of this simulation approach is that it does what we want it to: it does give more weight to recent data and less to older. There are also other advantages, crucial ones, but first there is a problem. We are still faced with the need to find estimates of A1 and A2 to begin the simulation.

   It has been proved that if the simulation is started with A1 and A2 equal to the nonweighted least-squares values, the result will be exactly the weighted least-squares values. With a computer it is easy and inexpensive to go through the process of (1) finding the ordinary least-squares values, (2) simulating the exponential updating, and (3) finding the values A1 and

A2 which would be produced by the formulas shown in the previous section anyway. But why bother? Why is simulation useful at all?

The answer is that simulation is useful precisely because it is not a one-step, statistical-formula process. If a computer program is used to perform the simulation, it can also check for a wide variety of error conditions at each step in the process, and noting such conditions can be crucial.

The two most important kinds of error conditions are:

Outliers, values so high or so low that they should be thrown out. If all data values but one are less than ten, and then a value of 1000 is encountered, obviously something is wrong. The outlier is probably the result of a clerical error, but even if it is factually valid it should not be counted on an equal basis with the other data. The Ruritanian tractors mentioned in Chapter 4 are a case in point.

Changes of pattern, such as major changes in level or a switch from declining values to an upward trend or *vice versa.* Changes like these can be recognized automatically by tracking signals, which are the subject of a later chapter.

Neither of these factors is satisfactorily dealt with by simply applying statistical formulas. (In fact, almost nothing can be correctly handled by blindly using formulas.) The first one could conceivably be handled without simulation, by simply throwing away any very high or low values, but the technique is a bit more difficult than it appears, and we shall return to it in another chapter. The second factor, changes of pattern, is even more difficult; it probably cannot be handled at all by modifying the standard formulas.

Specific methods which can be applied to the simulation will be described later. Because the error conditions mentioned above are a hazard in any model that relies on past data, they may be used in connection with any periodic updating procedure.

IS THERE REALLY A TREND?

One particular hazard applies specifically to trend models rather than all models, and is not detected by the error-checking procedures mentioned above. Once a computer program has been written to calculate level and trend, it is very easy to use. In fact, it is fun to use. As a result, it is sometimes used when it shouldn't be.

Even if there really is no trend in the data being analyzed, the fitting procedure will produce one. And if you base forecasts on this spurious trend, you will be in trouble. It is therefore worth checking trends to make certain they are real before using them.

If only a few items are being analyzed, you can prepare graphs and inspect them. You should be able to decide whether there is a trend, and then apply a trend-line or a level-only model as appropriate. But when you need a good many analyses, as in inventory control, market studies, demographic forecasting, and other areas, a routine and preferably computerized method is probably necessary.

Fortunately, one is already available. It is the null-hypothesis test method already introduced for determining the significance of correlations. A trend can be regarded as a correlation with time. If a trend is present, the data values should increase or decrease at some reasonably steady rate as the time values increase.

Testing for a trend by this method is quite easy. The variable T, mentioned in Fig. 3–3, is calculated as follows:

$$T = R\sqrt{\frac{N - 2}{1 - R^2}},$$

where R is the correlation coefficient of X (the data) and T (the time values). The T-variable can then be tested directly against tables of confidence limits.

If the variable under consideration actually does not have a trend, but only random variation around a steady horizontal value, the value of T will be between -2.306 and $+2.306$ 95% of the time. This means that if you calculate a trend, compute R, and then compute T, you can decide whether or not the trend is an accident due to normal variation in the data or actually represents an increase or decrease over time by simply checking whether T is between the two values indicated.

Exercise. Figure 5–15 is a graph of monthly paint brush usage in an industrial operation. Is there a trend? When the standard trend line calculation was made, it showed a trend of 0.74 and a level of 22 at time T1; calculate R. Calculate T; is it between -2.036 and $+2.306$? Is the apparent trend the result of random variation, or is it real?

Development of Pictorial Representation

There are several ways to improve on the graphic presentation of forecast errors that was introduced in Chapter 4. Figure 5–16 shows the results of two modifications. The graph has been tilted, so that the line of perfect forecasts is emphasized, and the dimensions now indicate forecast and actual *changes* rather than absolute numerical values. The first step just provides more convenience in reading the picture, but the second actually gives a more detailed analysis of a forecasting system's weaknesses.

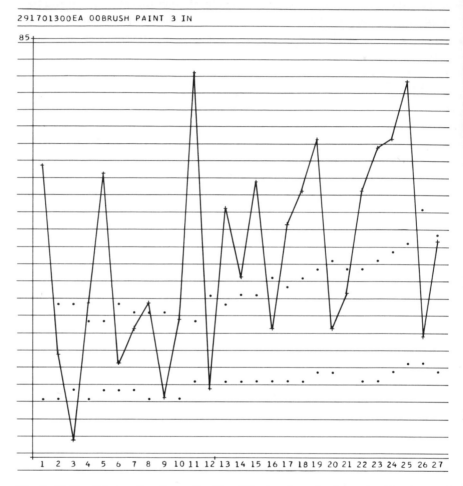

291701300EA 00BRUSH PAINT 3 IN

Fig. 5–15 Possibly trending item. Reality of the trend can be determined by the trend test based on finding the probability that this trend is the result of pure accident in a population that is, in fact, trendless.

SOME MORE CAUTIONS

Two points, one minor and one very important, remain to be made about the reality of trends. The minor point concerns the difference between theory and practice. Although using a trend model where there is no actual trend is

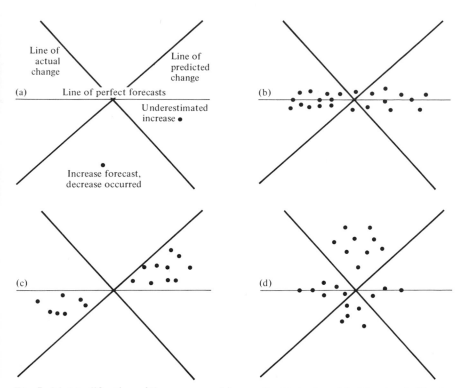

Fig. 5–16 Modification of the error-graphing method introduced in Chapter 4. Graph (a) shows the changes; graphs (b), (c), and (d) show possible results. One shows a system that underestimates changes, another shows a system that does not forecast changes in trend, and the remaining one shows a reasonably good system. Can you tell which is which?

wrong in theory, in practice it may be quite harmless. The forecast errors will be a few percent higher than otherwise, but this is acceptable in many circumstances. The test of acceptability is whether the error costs more than the human and computer time required to perform the trend test and eliminate it.

The major point is somewhat similar in theme, but more general. The statistical concept of goodness-of-fit, reflected in factors like the sum of the squared errors from the trend line, is not an appropriate standard for judging the value of a model. The only way to judge a trend model or any other model is to use it to forecast test values, and see whether the forecasts are better or worse than others. Even if the sum of the squared errors from the trend line is less than the sum of squared errors from the average, forecasts based on the trend model may still be less accurate than those produced by other models. In other words, whether or not there is a trend the basic question is still, "Does it work?" This subject will be returned to in detail in the final section of this book.

Exercise. If a factor is undergoing long-term growth or decline, as indicated above, the simple smoothed value will also grow or decline, but with some lag behind the actual values. What would happen if you smoothed the successive smoothed values? Would the resulting Double Smoothed Value (DSV) lag behind the Simple Smoothed Value (SSV)? Can you calculate the amount of lag, assuming a given fixed trend? What is the relationship of this lag to the lag of the SSV behind the actual values? Can you calculate the actual value of the trending factor from the SSV and the DSV together? Can you forecast the expected value using them? If you enjoyed high school algebra, show that this approach amounts to the same thing as the smoothed two-point differences method of handling trends described in this chapter.

A Random Walk Through the Market

The example used to illustrate correlation concepts in an earlier chapter was drawn from the stock market. Applying the correlation concept showed that about 73 % of the movement in IBM's price was "explained by" movements in the Dow Jones Industrials Average (DJIA) over the time period considered. This level of relatedness is characteristic of stock prices: they do tend to move together.

This is an interesting result, and it would be pleasant if equally interesting data led to a means of forecasting stock prices. For instance, market trends are obviously important. This suggests that a trend-type forecasting model would be appropriate for market prices. If the model described in this chapter applied, for instance, forecasters who knew how to use it would have an edge over other traders and would be able to get rich (quickly or slowly: either would be acceptable).

Extensive research in the forecasting of New York, American, and other stock exchange averages as well as commodity prices and the values of various indices has been carried out over the past several decades. The original pioneering work was carried out for French stocks by Louis Bachelier in the early 1900s. But market forecasting and strategy testing require so much arithmetic that they have become practical only since computers have been readily available. The most interesting work has been done only in the last decade, all of it by computer. A collection by Professor Paul Cootner*

---

* Cootner, Paul H. (ed.), *The Random Character of Stock Market Prices*, M.I.T. Press, Cambridge, 1964.

provides an excellent overview of the technical work, while the articles by "Adam Smith" which originally appeared in *New York* magazine, and were later collected and expanded into a book,* give a popular version which includes quite a few other thoughts on market-playing.

What the researchers discovered is basically that both individual-stock prices and the market as a whole are a "random walk." That is, the quantity $X(T) - X(T - 1)$ is a random variable. If you graph the frequency of various sizes of market change, you get the normal curve shown in Fig. 5–17. This indicates that the chance of the market going up next week is the same as its chance of going down.

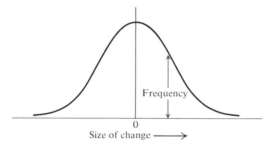

Fig. 5–17 A normal distribution, which describes the frequency of different sizes of market changes. The height of the curve indicates the frequency of the change shown on the horizontal axis; zero is the most likely change, small changes are much more frequent than large changes, and positive and negative changes occur in equal numbers. One school of analysts claims that this curve describes the actual distribution of day-to-day price changes on major exchanges.

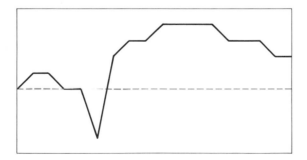

Fig. 5–18 An imitation stock-market price graph, made by choosing price changes at random from a normally distributed population. (Refer to Fig. 5–6.)

Figure 5–18 shows a graph constructed by (1) producing a series of values from a normal random distribution, and (2) graphing their sum by

---

* "Smith, Adam," *The Money Game*, Dell, N.Y., 1967.

adding or subtracting from the current value. It looks remarkably like a market chart, and is indeed statistically almost identical.

Exercise. Try it yourself. One way to get a normally distributed series of random numbers is to flip a coin ten times, count the number of heads, and subtract five. This gives you your first value. For instance, seven heads gives a value of two. Repeat for more values and graph the result.

In other words, test after test seems to confirm that "the market has no memory." The statisticians say that a rise or a fall in prices is equally likely at any point, and the direction of change last week has no influence on the direction or amount of change this week. This completely contradicts the popular image of the market as a bull or a bear, consistently rising or falling over a given period. And what about those market charts showing long periods of rise followed by long periods of decline, or the reverse?

Actually, there is some statistical structure to the market's procedure, but it is so insignificant that it will never make you rich. There are three main deviations from a true statistical random walk:

1. It is more accurate to say that the percentage change, rather than the numerical change, is normally distributed. The random variable is thus either $X(T) - X(T - 1)/X(T - 1)$ or the logarithm of the change, $LOG(X(T) - X(T - 1))$. This implies that the market values themselves are distributed in a log-normal fashion; this distribution is discussed in the chapter on curved forecasting patterns.

2. There is a very slight amount of "memory" present, and trends last a bit longer than they would if the distribution were truly random. In technical terms, the autocorrelation of the series of values is not zero. However, the value of the autocorrelation is obviously related to the length of the interval between measurements. For weekly data, it is very slightly negative, while for daily values it is slightly positive. This slight persistence of pattern has led some analysts to develop the idea of a "filter": buying whenever the price goes down a certain percentage of its former value, and selling whenever it goes up the same percentage. However, experience shows that the profit to be made from this system, while it exists, is so small that it will not make up for the commissions you pay on your trades. If you don't pay commission, of course, you can improve your performance, but that's cheating.

3. There are rather more very large and very small changes, and fewer medium-sized changes, than a pure normal curve would produce. The

differences, again, are so small that they would not show up on a diagram that would fit on this page.

Full-scale simulation models of market behavior are just beginning to be developed. They may provide a more accurate picture than simple trend models can, but early indications are that they aren't much better than human forecasts. And human forecasts are not all that good, even with statistical help. Mazuy and Treynor conducted a study* which proved that mutual fund selections performed about as well as a totally random portfolio.

So far, then, the results of attempts to forecast stock prices by trend or other models have been rather negative. But that does not mean that price forecasting cannot be done successfully. It just means that nobody has done it yet.

---

* Mazuy, Kay K., and Jack L. Treynor, "Can Mutual Funds Outguess the Market?" *Harvard Business Review,* **44,** No. 4 (July–August, 1966), p. 113ff. Also described in Benton, W. K., *The Use of the Computer in Planning,* Addison-Wesley, Reading, Mass., 1971.

CHAPTER 6

SEASONALITY AND CURVATURE

The simple forecasting model of the previous chapters, which involved only a level of activity and an upward or downward trend, is obviously not suited for all types of forecasting. Figure 6–1 shows monthly-usage graphs of truck supply items at one of the world's largest mining operations. Usages for 24 successive months are shown, and it is clear that there is more structure to the pattern of usages than simply a level and a trend, or even a trend that is changing. At a certain part of the year in each case, usage is in general higher than for the rest of the year. This effect of time of year on the value of a time series like those shown is called *seasonality*. It is fundamentally different from a trend line model because the effect shown is cyclic, returning each year at about the same time, rather than being pervasive through a long time period as a simple trend is.

Another example of a pattern that can't be described by a trend line is long-term sales growth for most products, and size growth for corporations and other organizations. Growth here tends to rise in an accelerated curve; for this reason, among others, sales and population growth are usually described in percentage increases rather than dollar or unit increases. A stable percentage increase each month or year produces the upward curve shown in Fig. 6–2. A repeated decline of the same percentage produces the downward curve.

These curves generally apply to medium-term time scales, which cover a major portion of the life history of a product or a population. They do not, however, cover the entire span. If a long term rather than a medium-term view is taken, the curvature usually changes. There is typically an initial acceleration phase, followed by a leveling-off or even a declining phase. Patterns of this sort can be described by S-shaped curves like those shown in Fig. 6–3.

The most effective way to deal with seasonal patterns, curvature, and similar models, is to describe the model in terms of constant parameters, and then to estimate and update these parameters in the usual exponential smoothing fashion. This approach has already been applied to the trend

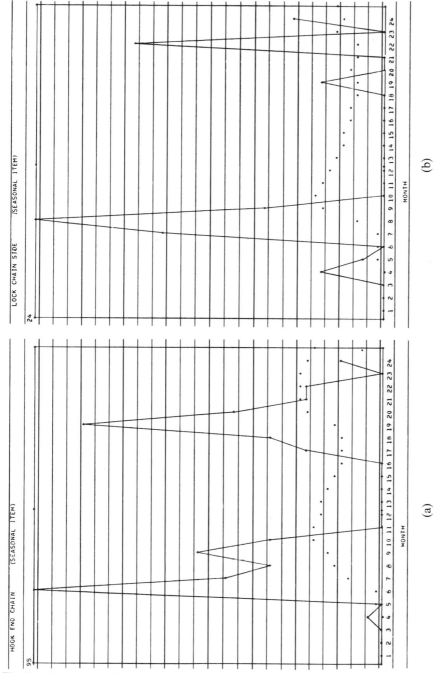

Fig. 6–1 Parts (a) and (b) represent examples of data with cyclical or seasonal variations, and illustrate the inadequacy of the simple updated trend model for some types of data. The dotted line shows the forecasts made by this model; obviously it does not reflect the large short-term variation accurately, and a new kind of model is called for.

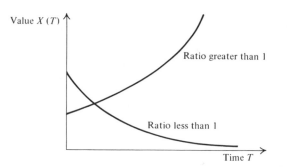

Fig. 6–2 Typical percentage growth curves. Ratio = X(T)/X(T − 1).

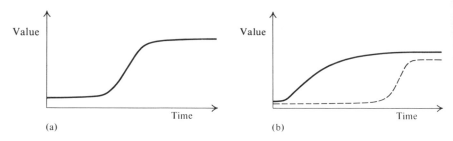

Fig. 6–3 Examples of changing curvature.

model, which involved two parameters, namely, the level A1 and the trend A2.

For patterns that involve some departure from the straightforward trend we need another parameter—some measure of that departure. For simple upward or downward moving curves, the parameter of interest is the ratio of each value to the preceding value. In symbols, this is $X(T)/X(T − 1)$. This ratio is larger than one for increasing curves, and smaller than one for decreasing curves. For S-shaped curves, two parameters are needed to specify a particular shape.

For all of these curves, once the parameters that specify the best curve have been estimated, they can be updated as new information becomes available, in the same way that level and trend are updated in the trend model. For instance, when a new month's sales figures become available for a seasonal item, it is easy to calculate the ratio of the actual sales to the figure forecast by a trend line. This ratio can then be used to improve the estimate of the seasonal ratio for that month, and the resulting updated ratio can be used to forecast the value for next year. The same applies to curved models, S-shaped models, and almost every other type of model which is useful in management. For simple accelerated curves, a by-product of this method is a particularly neat way of finding maximum and minimum likely values; this method is discussed in the next chapter.

SEASONALITY: THE BASIC IDEA

The simplest way to deal with seasonality is to compare the value of the variable at each month or other time period against an overall average value for the year or for the entire process. The average can be represented by the fitted straight line through the data. Then for each time period, the ratio of the actual value observed to the value of the trend line can be used as a measure of the seasonality, that is, present.

This ratio, the comparison of the "abnormal" to the "normal" value, is called the base index, and it is the parameter we want to find. We calculate it by simply fitting the trend line, as described in earlier chapters, and dividing the actual value for a given period by the corresponding trend-line value. If you have more than one year's worth of actual data, the ratios for corresponding months can be averaged together.

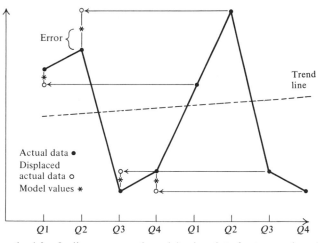

Fig. 6–4 A method for finding a seasonal model using data for two cycles. Actual data values for the same period of successive cycles are averaged—they are estimates of the true seasonal values. The deviation of the actual data from these model values estimates the importance of the seasonal effect.

For instance, in the graph shown in Fig. 6–4 there are two years of data. In both first quarters, the actual value is high compared to the trend line; both first quarter ratios are more than one. In fact, the ratios are $23/15 = 1.53$ and $21/17 = 1.23$, or an average of 1.38. The seasonal index for the first quarter is therefore 1.38. The forecast for the next year's first quarter can then be found by extrapolating the trend line and multiplying its first quarter value by 1.38. Since the extrapolated trend line's value is 19 for the first quarter the following year, the forecast is 1.38∗, 19, or 26.2.

The forecast for each part of the year can be found by the same method, finding the appropriate monthly base index and using it to modify the trend forecast. In this particular example, the base indices are higher than 1.0 at the beginning of the year and lower at the end. The corresponding forecasts are shown in Fig. 6–5.

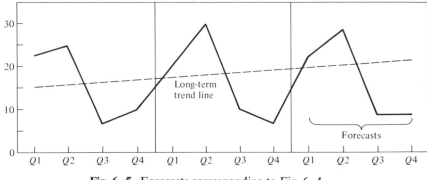

Fig. 6–5 Forecasts corresponding to Fig. 6–4.

The base index approach can, of course, be applied to cyclic variation over any time period. If your business at the beginning of the month is different from that at the end, or if it's different in the morning and the afternoon, the same idea can be used. The only thing that would change would be the period of measurement; you might have weekly or hourly indices instead of monthly or quarterly ones.

We obtained the initial base indices by using one year's actual figures, or by taking a simple average (arithmetic mean) of data from more than one year. But seasonality can change just as every other factor can; increased spendable income might increase the number of winter vacations and cruises taken and make beachwear a year-round item, for instance. So we will want to update the base indices as new information becomes available. This can be done by exponential smoothing, in the same way we update level and trend.

Why Identify Seasonality?

There are certain obvious time series which are seasonal. Sales of toys, for instance, are much higher just before Christmas than they are during the rest of the year. Sales of skis are higher in the fall than in the spring, and sales of bathing suits are the reverse.

But sometimes such obvious things are not at all as obvious as they seem. One forecasting project investigated the application of seasonality measures to the items used in servicing a fleet of trucks. Some things like snow tires were definitely seasonal, and others, like gasoline, were definitely nonseasonal. At the beginning of the project the team discussed antifreeze as a typical seasonal item which should be appropriately handled by the seasonal forecasting system. About two months after the project began, historical data on actual usage became available. To everyone's surprise, antifreeze was not seasonal at all. Inquiry produced the information that mechanics kept the trucks filled with antifreeze all year long because it reduced corrosion in the radiators! There is an obvious moral to the tale: never assume anything.

The immense scale of operations in modern business and government often means that thousands or hundreds of thousands of items must be investigated for seasonality. Without a computer routine, the task would be impossible: the numbers involved are so great that individual review by administrators or technical people is out of the question. But another question might be asked. Why bother to identify seasonality at all?

Why not assume that every item is seasonal, and always use a seasonal model? After all, if there is, in fact, no seasonal effect, all the indices will automatically be set equal to or very near 1.0, so they should have no net impact. Nothing seems to be lost by assuming seasonality, except perhaps a few extra seconds of computer time.

The answer is that sometimes this assumption produces disastrous errors. In the case of the truck fleet study, seasonality analyses were prepared for all the items in a large sample of spare parts, and forecasts were prepared on the basis of these analyses. Many of the forecasts for nonseasonal items turned out to be wildly high or even negative. The reason was occasional unusual usages. If all the carburetors in the fleet had been replaced at one point as routine maintenance, carburetor usage for that month would be unusually high. The computer, in its mechanical, unthinking way, would therefore calculate an unusually high seasonality factor for that month, and the result would be an enormous forecast for that month the following year, when high usage was, in fact, not expected. Placing orders for enough carburetors to cover the erroneous forecast would cause turmoil.

This possibility is similar, again, to the Ruritanian tractor order: an unusual event disrupting future forecasts. But with seasonality the problem is likely to cause more trouble, for two reasons. The original outlier is less likely to be noticed because seasonal values are by definition variable, and the results of the error will not show up until the next year (or other cycle), when everyone is likely to have forgotten what caused them. The turmoil mentioned above is then likely to be name-calling directed at the computer and its keepers. It is worth performing one of the simple seasonality tests described in the next section to prevent this, even at some cost to the efficiency of computer operations.

Measuring Seasonality

Suppose you have two years' worth of sales data that looks like the curve in Figs. 6–4 and 6–6. It certainly looks seasonal: sales for the first two quarters of each year are much higher than for the last two. But how can you tell for sure? How can you put numbers on it?

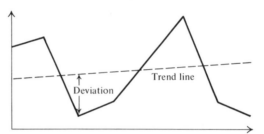

Fig. 6–6 For seasonal data, deviations between the trend line and the actual values are fairly large. They are much larger than those between the actual values and the seasonal model shown in Fig. 6–5. The ratio of the average absolute deviation for the trend model to that of the seasonal model is quite high, marking the data as clearly seasonal. The ratio can be found by computer.

The figure suggests a simple method. You construct a seasonal model of the data and measure it for accuracy, and then do the same for a simple trend model. If the seasonal model is much closer to the actual data when you compare the mean absolute deviations (MADs) of the two models, you can reasonably conclude that the item is seasonal.

With more than one year's data, you can construct a simple seasonal model by averaging together all first-quarter data, then all second-quarter data, and so on. This gives you one value for each quarter. The overall accuracy of this model can be measured by finding all the absolute deviations of the actual values from the model values, and averaging them. This is the seasonal-model MAD. The trend-line model can be fitted by the least-squares method, and deviations found and used to calculate the trend-model

MAD. The smaller MAD will then indicate the more accurate model, *if* the difference is large enough.

Exercise 1. For the data given in Fig. 6–5, which is larger, the seasonal-model MAD or the trend-model MAD?

Exercise 2. The average deviation of the first two quarter-values from the seasonal model is equal to half their difference. That is, it equals $(X5 - X1)/2$. Why?

In general, seasonality is present if the ratio of the trend-model MAD to the seasonal-model MAD is over 2.0. For the data in the example, the ratio is about 4.

This method is a standard one, and works quite well. It is easy to understand, and easy to program for computer use. But several other methods can also be conceived, and one of them seems to be slightly more sensitive to small degrees of seasonality. This method relies on the idea that, if seasonality is present, high values in a given part of the cycle will be associated with high values in the same part at later times. For example, a high first-quarter value in one year should be associated with a high first-quarter value in the second year. If the data are not seasonal, there is no such association.

You can detect this state of affairs by averaging together all first-quarter values, all second-quarter values, and so on, and then comparing the results with the overall average of the data. If the quarterly averages are near the overall average, the item probably is not seasonal. This is because for non-seasonal items high and low values for each quarter as well as for the entire year will tend to cancel out during the averaging process. On the other hand, if the quarter average is very far from the overall average, the item is seasonal; the canceling has not taken place. Finally, if the item is seasonal, the quarterly averages will be widely scattered: some will be very high, some will be very low. And *their* MAD will therefore be high, compared to the overall average. It will be higher than the MAD which would be expected from simply averaging together pairs of values from nonseasonal data. If the MAD of the quarterly averages is more than 1.4 times that of the overall average, seasonality is indicated. This value is based on experience; a more exact statistical value can also be found.

Finally, as you might have guessed from the premise of the last method, seasonality can also be identified by correlation. After all, seasonality means that high or low values in one period are associated with similar values in the corresponding period four quarters, 12 months, 52 weeks, or some other appropriate interval later. So a correlation analysis of the data points $X(T)$ with points $X(T + 4)$ should identify seasonality if the data are quarterly.

The standard significance tests can then be applied directly to deal with marginal cases where the result is near the dividing value of 2.0. Of course, two years' worth of quarterly data will give only four pairs for correlation analysis, and this is not enough for meaningful analysis; correlation is therefore a bit limited by the need for a large number of data points. Two years' worth of monthly data, however, will be adequate.

Exercise 3. In measuring seasonality, should you use a weighted trend line or an unweighted one as the central line? Is an unweighted trend line the same as a regression line with time as the independent variable?

How Well Does It Work?

Figure 6–7 is a graph of an inventory item identified as seasonal by a program like those described above. The graph shows that this particular item is strongly seasonal. Until the program was run, however, this item was handled just like any other level or trend item in the firm's inventory.

The item had been buried in masses of data which could not be reviewed manually. This was a manufacturing item, and about $400 worth per year was used. The trend line forecast for the third year produced an average error of about 230%. The seasonal index system reduced this average error to about 68%, clearly a major improvement.

The item was only one of a group of 50 sample items from the manufacturer's production supplies inventory. The sample was chosen so that each item corresponded to about 500 in the entire operation. The seasonality identification program also pointed out six other sample items as mildly seasonal; some of these graphs are shown in Fig. 6–8. For these items the seasonality was less obvious to the eye, and the accuracy of the forecast based on the trend line was just about the same as that of the seasonal forecasts. However, the saving of inventory investment in the one seasonal item in the sample, and in the far larger number it indicated for the overall operation, fully justified the cost of handling them with a separate seasonal program.

If you suspect that seasonality is a factor to be reckoned with in your forecasts, you can test its applicability in several ways. First, you can simply try it out. This is the simulation approach discussed earlier in reference to determining if there is actually a trend. If you have enough information to calculate the seasonal coefficients, and still have data left over, you can forecast values for a year ahead. You can then compare these forecast values with the actual subsequent values.

260362639EA 00SWITCH INST PANEL TG 0003094 HAULPAK

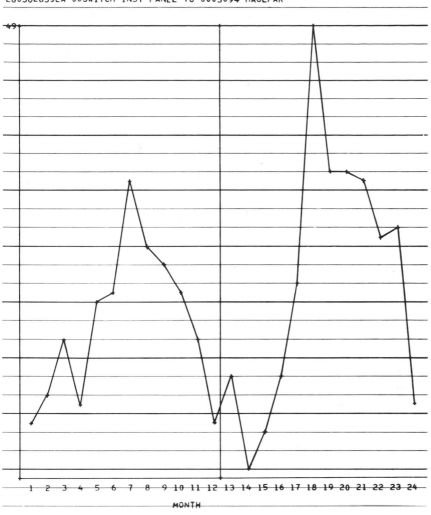

Fig. 6–7 Item identified by computer as seasonal.

However, this is not really enough. Even if the seasonal forecasts are reasonably close to the subsequent actual values, that does not mean that they are closer than the ones a simpler model might give you. To find out, you will have to go through the same procedure for either simple exponential smoothing or a trend line. You can then compare the accuracy of the two types of forecasts, and see whether adding seasonality has improved the forecast.

222514004TON21POWDER AMMONIUM NITRATE BULK

MONTH

Fig. 6–8a Parts (a), (b), and (c) represent items identified by computer as tentatively seasonal.

This procedure is illustrated by the analysis in Fig. 6–9. These are usages of an item for which two years and three months of data were available when the analysis was done. Seasonal indices were calculated for each month on the basis of the first two years' data. Then the indices were used to forecast expected values for each of the next three months. The three actual data points were then compared against the seasonal forecast. The same pro-

255627806EA 00SPARK PLUG NO J8 CHAMPION

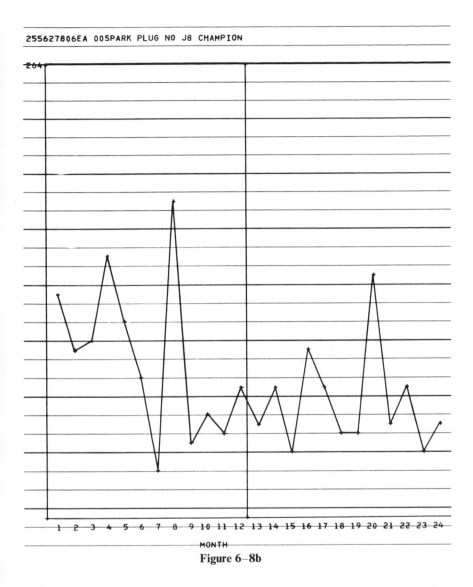

MONTH

Figure 6–8b

cedure was carried out for the trend line forecasts. The result was three number series for each item: the forecasts for the first three months of the third year on the basis of the seasonal model and on the basis of the trend line, and the actual three-month usages.

This three-way comparison may seem unwieldy and time-consuming, but it is not quite that bad. The trend line must be calculated in any case, when the seasonal forecasts are begun. The only additional work is actually

260040540EA 00STUD WHEEL LUG 22 0002188 KENW

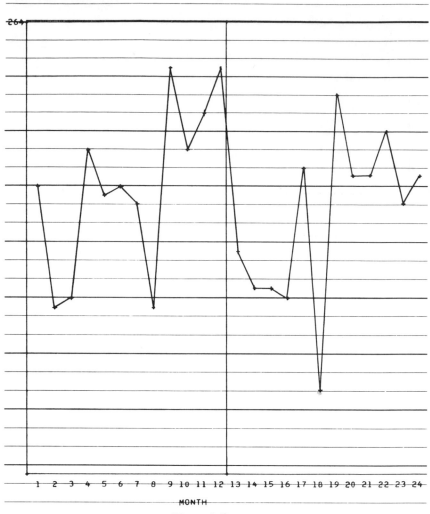

Figure 6–8c

printing the forecasts for the trend line. The same set of steps is used to measure the accuracy of both types of forecast, and the computer routine need be written only once. Since this is a one-time comparison for each item, the slight increase in computer running time is a negligible cost, more than justified by the savings on more accurate forecasts in future.

However, it is all a little more complicated than necessary. This method is of interest to human reviewers and analysts, and can be used to advantage

```
FORECAST ANALYSIS FOR 2615697458A 48TIRE 2100     9 36 PLY XTRED
   ANNUAL USAGE   185 UNITS
   PRICE $ 1879.650
   SERVICE LEVEL 3
   LEADTIME (DAYS)   138
   LEADTIME VARIABILITY     0 UNITS

INITIALIZING DATA
  15.0   13.0   20.0   14.0   24.0    9.0
  22.0   12.0   12.0   19.0   16.0   26.0
   9.0   26.0   18.0    8.0   23.0   17.0
   8.0   16.0    9.0   15.0   14.0   17.0


LEVEL AND TREND AT TIME 1   17.0   -.1
SEASONAL INDICES
1.01  1.08  1.05  1.00  1.11  1.01  .89  .85  .83  .95  1.10  1.12

ACTUAL VALUES   26   12   20
```

MO	ACT	LVL	TREND	TREND FCST	ERR	INDEX	SEASONAL FCST	ERR	INDICES													ACT/TL
1	26.0	14.7	-.1	14.6	11.4	1.0	14.8	11.2	1.0	1.1	1.0	1.0	1.1	1.0	.9	.9	.8	.9	1.1	1.1		1.78
2	12.0	15.8	.5	16.2	-4.2	1.1	18.7	-6.7	1.2	1.1	1.0	1.0	1.1	1.0	.9	.9	.8	.9	1.1	1.1		.74
3	20.0	15.8	.3	16.1	3.9	1.0	16.4	3.6	1.1	1.1	1.1	1.0	1.0	1.0	.9	.9	.8	.9	1.1	1.1		1.24
4	16	16	0	17			17.3		1.1	1.1	1.1	1.0	1.0	1.0	.9	.9	.8	.9	1.1	1.1		

Note updated seasonal index based on new observed ratio of 1.78.

Used in updating seasonal index.

```
AVERAGE PERCENT ERROR
   TPEND    32.894
   SEASONAL 38.952
```

Fig. 6–9 Three-way comparison of actual data (ACT), trend forecasts (TREND FCST), and seasonal forecasts (SEASONAL FCST). The forecasts are all based entirely on earlier data, but are updated for each actual value.

when presenting results to nontechnical audiences. But more direct statistical methods can and should be used when large numbers of items and long time periods are being evaluated for seasonality. General exponential smoothing, discussed in the section after next, is one of these methods.

Updating Seasonality

The very simple approach to updating seasonal (or base) indices which was used in the program that produced Fig. 6–12 can be improved upon. The method used there amounts to updating the index for a given period of the total cycle (January, for instance) every time that period occurs, but *not* updating the level (and possibly trend) at the same time. In seasonal models the level is intended to be a stable, central value throughout the entire cycle. If the level is updated in the portion of the cycle that is higher than average, it will end up being itself higher than average; if the high part of the cycle is followed by a lower-than-average portion, the smoothed level will then follow the data down. The smoothed value, in short, will not really be a stable central value to which the actual values can be compared. Instead, it will be a kind of shadow of the actual cyclic data, as suggested in Fig. 6–10.

This problem can be avoided by updating the central level only once in each complete cycle. But when information is in short supply and rapid correction is needed, a method which makes use of all figures as they become available would be much better. There is such a method, and its basic idea is shown in Fig. 6–11.

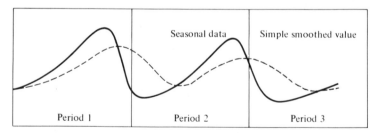

Fig. 6–10 The effect of seasonal patterns on the simple smoothed value (SSV) based on the seasonal data. As suggested in the sketch, the SSV is a lagging, attenuated shadow of the original data. As a result, the SSV is not an appropriate statistic either for forecasting seasonal patterns or for estimating the central or average level of a seasonal variable. The text explains a means of measuring the central value; it also describes a way to relate the seasonal values to the central level and a way to update both of them.

The seasonal index for a particular part of any cycle is the ratio of the expected actual value to the central value for the entire pattern. The circled items in the diagram are data items used in updating, and the boxes represent the calculations of new values.

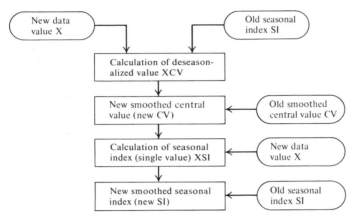

Fig. 6–11 Steps in updating the central value of a seasonal pattern (CV) and the seasonal indices (SI).

The diagram can be translated into the following set of formulas, using the notation shown in the diagram:

$$XCV = X/\text{old SI}$$
$$\text{new CV} = \text{old CV} + H*(XCV - \text{old CV}).$$
$$XSI = X/\text{new CV}$$
$$\text{new SI} = \text{old SI} + H*(XSI - \text{old SI}).$$

Both the diagram and the equations indicate that the new data value and the old seasonal ratio are used to produce a new central value observation. This in turn is used to update the central value estimate, by smoothing, and to create a new ratio observation. The new ratio observation is then used to update the seasonal index by smoothing. It's not as complicated as it sounds; the new observation is just reflected back and forth between the central value and the ratio, and smoothed with the old values of both.

This procedure can easily be translated into a computer program (Fig. 6–12), and performed at each observation-point in the cycle. There is, of course, a different SI for each part of the cycle—month, quarter, or what have you. Since most seasonal situations are annual rather than monthly or weekly, this immediate updating provides needed information where otherwise there would be a long delay and perhaps serious consequences.

Exercise. If you are dealing with seasonal data on a monthly basis, why not carry 12 values? Have a separate series for each month and use simple

UPDATING OF SEASONAL INDICES
WEEKLY CYCLE

STARTING INDICES

1.00	1.00	1.00	1.00	1.00	1.00	1.00

ONE WEEK DAILY DATA

50.00	60.00	70.00	80.00	10.00	120.00	100.00

DAY	DATA	CENTRAL VALUE OLD	UPDATED	SEASONAL INDICES --- (UPDATED)						
1	50.	100.00	95.00	0.86	1.00	1.00	1.00	1.00	1.00	1.00
2	60.	95.00	91.50	0.86	0.90	1.00	1.00	1.00	1.00	1.00
3	70.	91.50	89.35	0.86	0.90	0.94	1.00	1.00	1.00	1.00
4	80.	89.35	88.41	0.86	0.90	0.94	0.97	1.00	1.00	1.00
5	110.	88.41	90.57	0.86	0.90	0.94	0.97	1.06	1.00	1.00
6	120.	90.57	93.52	0.86	0.90	0.94	0.97	1.06	1.08	1.00
7	100.	93.52	94.16	0.86	0.90	0.94	0.97	1.06	1.08	1.02
1	50.	94.16	90.58	0.77	0.90	0.94	0.97	1.06	1.08	1.02
2	60.	90.58	88.21	0.77	0.83	0.94	0.97	1.06	1.08	1.02
3	70.	88.21	86.88	0.77	0.83	0.90	0.97	1.06	1.08	1.02
4	80.	86.88	86.42	0.77	0.83	0.90	0.96	1.06	1.08	1.02
5	110.	86.42	88.12	0.77	0.83	0.90	0.96	1.12	1.08	1.02
6	120.	88.12	90.36	0.77	0.83	0.90	0.96	1.12	1.16	1.02
7	100.	90.36	91.15	0.77	0.83	0.90	0.96	1.12	1.16	1.04
1	50.	91.15	88.56	0.71	0.83	0.90	0.96	1.12	1.16	1.04
2	60.	88.56	86.91	0.71	0.79	0.90	0.96	1.12	1.16	1.04
3	70.	86.91	86.03	0.71	0.79	0.87	0.96	1.12	1.16	1.04
4	80.	86.03	85.78	0.71	0.79	0.87	0.95	1.12	1.16	1.04
5	110.	85.78	87.03	0.71	0.79	0.87	0.95	1.16	1.16	1.04
6	120.	87.03	88.69	0.71	0.79	0.87	0.95	1.16	1.22	1.04
7	100.	88.69	89.42	0.71	0.79	0.87	0.95	1.16	1.22	1.07
1	50.	89.42	87.56	0.67	0.79	0.87	0.95	1.16	1.22	1.07
2	60.	87.56	86.41	0.67	0.76	0.87	0.95	1.16	1.22	1.07
3	70.	86.41	85.80	0.67	0.76	0.85	0.95	1.16	1.22	1.07
4	80.	85.80	85.64	0.67	0.76	0.85	0.95	1.16	1.22	1.07
5	110.	85.64	86.53	0.67	0.76	0.85	0.95	1.20	1.22	1.07
6	120.	86.53	87.75	0.67	0.76	0.85	0.95	1.20	1.26	1.07
7	100.	87.75	88.36	0.67	0.76	0.85	0.95	1.20	1.26	1.09
1	50.	88.36	87.04	0.64	0.76	0.85	0.95	1.20	1.26	1.09
2	60.	87.04	86.22	0.64	0.74	0.85	0.95	1.20	1.26	1.09
3	70.	86.22	85.79	0.64	0.74	0.84	0.95	1.20	1.26	1.09
4	80.	85.79	85.67	0.64	0.74	0.84	0.94	1.20	1.26	1.09
5	110.	85.67	86.31	0.64	0.74	0.84	0.94	1.22	1.26	1.09
6	120.	86.31	87.19	0.64	0.74	0.84	0.94	1.22	1.30	1.09
7	100.	87.19	87.68	0.64	0.74	0.84	0.94	1.22	1.30	1.10

Fig. 6–12 Example of updating seasonal indices. In this example, each day of the week has its own seasonal index. The data might be sales in a store; it is assumed that the sales pattern for each week is identical. The seasonal indices all start off at 1.0; the updating procedure causes them to move toward the actual ratio of sales to the average and at the same time updates the average sales figures to a level more representative than the original value.

smoothing. One problem is that more memory space may be needed; base indices are usually less than 2.0, but the actual data values can be any size. Aside from file space savings, does the base index approach have any advantage over this simpler method?

General Exponential Smoothing

Some of the most basic and powerful concepts in mathematics are related to the sine curve. Figure 6–13 shows some typical curves. Sine curves occur in almost every part of nature: the height of an ocean wave, the strength of cyclic electrical current, and the height above the ground of an object moving in a vertical circle are only a few examples. There are also interesting mathematical models which result in sine curves. The most relevant of these is the situation in which deviations from some central value are corrected by a force which varies directly with the size of the deviation. The commonest example is an ordinary wire spring. If you squeeze or stretch it, it resists, and the strength of the resistance is proportional to the distance you have squeezed or stretched it. If you let it go, and graph its length as it oscillates, the result is a damped sine curve.

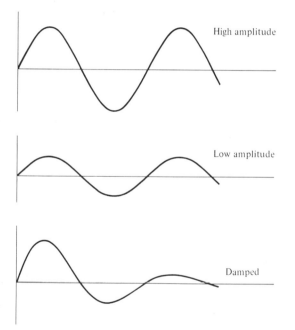

High amplitude

Low amplitude

Damped

Fig. 6–13 Typical sine curves.

There is no obvious reason that sine curves should apply to seasonality. Seasonal usages aren't caused by a deviation-correcting process; they are related to weather and holidays. But sine curves have been extensively studied by mathematicians, and they do provide good approximations to other kinds of cyclical data. In fact, any cycle can be expressed as the sum of a number of different sine curves, plus a trend if necessary. Procedures for fitting a few sine curves to seasonal data have been developed, and are the basis of some computer programs for handling seasonality, such as Arthur D. Little, Inc.'s System of Computations for Adaptively Revising Forecasts (SCARF). The method is known as general exponential smoothing, and it is extremely appealing to the mathematical mind.

The method works well if the seasonality is quite regular. One test compared simple smoothing, general exponential smoothing, and the base index approach, using three years' data on orders for drug items. When the model was fitted on years 1 and 2, and tested on year 3, the test showed that the general exponential method was more accurate than the simple smoothing. But it is *not* more accurate than the base index approach, and it is a lot more difficult. Moreover, if there is much random variation in the data the method tends to introduce large errors. This is because it finds a least-squares fit through the data of a sine curve model. If the data are very variable, there will occasionally be very high values. These will not be discarded by the screening process used for outlier detection, which we will discuss again in the next chapter, because the data in general are variable and the screening value must therefore be high. But the fitting procedure will arrange for the sine curve to pass close to the high value. This peak in the sine curve will be repeated in future years' forecasts, which is natural, but probably not quite accurate. Moreover, since the sine curve is symmetrical, the peak will be compensated for by a very low value somewhere else in the model. This too will probably reflect some degree of reality, but the result of these two factors is a wide range of variation in the forecasts.

This method is therefore not recommended for use with inventory or sales data unless the variability is very low. However, study of the concepts involved, which can be pursued in any statistics text, is highly recommended for the insights they afford into both forecasting models themselves and effective computer modeling. The subject is especially interesting if you know the basic concepts of vector or matrix algebra. But, as always, care must be exercised that the intellectual appeal of this model does not overshadow the practical problems in using it.

ACCELERATION, DECELERATION, AND CURVATURE

Figure 6–14 shows the annual sales of a large manufacturing company. Obviously neither a trend-line model nor a seasonal model fits the pattern of growth shown. Instead of rising gradually at a constant rate, or moving up and down cyclically, the sales are rising at an accelerated rate. This section is devoted to models which show acceleration, deceleration, or combinations of the two.

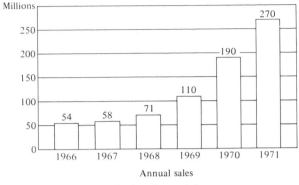

Fig. 6–14 Accelerated data.

We recognize that the accelerated model is appropriate in some circumstances when we make statements like, "Sales are rising 15% annually," or "Our share of the market is going down by 5% a year." If a trend model were appropriate for the circumstances, the sentences would read differently. The first would be something like, "Sales are increasing by $100,000 per year," naming a trend instead of a percentage increase. Using a percentage implicitly denotes a ratio type of model, accelerating upward or downward. While the percentage figure remains the same, the actual value it represents becomes larger or smaller as the base figure grows or declines, magnifying the upward or downward effect.

The Basic Idea

There are several ways to deal with this type of curvature. All of them convert the data which show curvature into a corresponding set of data which can be represented by a trend line or other simple model. The transformation of the original data into the corresponding set of simpler data is the key to dealing with all types of curved patterns. One way to do this is to compute the ratio of each data value to the previous value. The result is a series of numbers which is equivalent to the original series in the sense that it was derived from the original data points in a clear and unambiguous way. The corresponding series, of course, has one less data point than the original, since there is no "previous" value for the first point.

This method has a very useful property: if the original series really is accelerated on a percentage basis, all the values in the corresponding series of ratios are the same, or nearly so. For instance, the ratios for the sales figures graphed in Fig. 6–14 are

$$1.08,\ 1.20,\ 1.62,\ 1.76,\ 1.44.$$

If you graph these values, they will fall nearly on a horizontal line. You can then estimate, either visually from the graph or by taking an arithmetic average, what the average percentage increase is. This average ratio can be used to extrapolate future values by simple multiplication. In the example, the increase is about 40%. Multiplying the last sales figure by 140%, then, gives you next year's forecast, and multiplying that in turn by 140% gives you the forecast for the following year. Or, if the ratios themselves seem to be changing in a particular direction, as in the first four points in the example, you can use a trend line to estimate the change and use an increasing (or decreasing) percentage for every future year.

As new sales figures are obtained, of course, the average ratio should be updated. This is done just as for any other estimate, by applying simple exponential smoothing to the new values in combination with the old.

Other Types of Transformation

Relating a curved series of data points to each other as described above produces a corresponding series of ratios. These can then be treated as the values of a variable, and can be handled by simple smoothing, trend extrapolation, or seasonal analysis, where appropriate, just like any other data. The method is simple to use, readily comprehensible, and representative of many types of sales forecasting situations. It is not sophisticated at all, but there is usually so much random variation in sales figures that more sophisticated types of analysis are not warranted anyway.

This last point, however, is less true for very long-term sales forecasting. There, random variations are overshadowed by the longer-term processes at work. Other types of transformations are often useful for forecasts which span more than a few years. For instance, the original values may be replaced by their logarithms, by their square roots, or by their squares. Each of these has distinct advantages, but by far the most common transformation is the logarithmic one, in which each value is replaced by its logarithm, or *log*. This can be done easily by computer, since nearly all machines come with manufacturer-supplied log-finding programs.

When you fit a trend line to the logarithms of a series and extrapolate it, you get exactly the same result as you would have by finding the ratios and forecasting by using the average ratio. This is because a change in log values, by definition, corresponds to a multiplication; a constant trend in logs corresponds to a series of multiplications by some constant ratio. The main advantage of the log transformation is that graph paper is available with a vertical scale in logarithms rather than in constant units. If known data are graphed on this paper and a trend line is then drawn and extrapolated, the future values of the accelerated increase or decrease can be read off from the margin of the graph. Many highly sophisticated ways of using graphs like these have been developed, and sophisticated computers with plotting devices can make use of them; but they are really holdovers from precomputer methodology, and make better toys for engineers than tools for forecasters. There is certainly nothing wrong with using them, but there is no need to bother learning how if you don't already know.

The square and exponential transforms are suitable for dealing with a curve which is rising, but at a gradually decreasing rate, like that in Fig. 6–15. The object of these transforms, like that of the ratio transform, is to convert curved data into a trend-line series. The second graph in Fig. 6–15 shows the result of using the square transform: the new series consists of the squared values of the original data points. Squaring is just one variety of exponential transformation, using the exponent two. Other exponents can also be used where appropriate, including the data value itself. This one, of course, results in a curve which rises much more steeply than the progression of squares or any other simple exponential series. The general form is $Y = A * B^X$, where X is the data value.

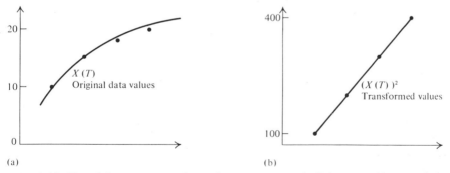

(a)

(b)

Fig. 6–15 Use of the square transformation to convert a declining rate of increase into trend-line data. Other powers besides two can be used.

The general procedure for using any of these transforms is the same:

1. Transform the original data to get a new series which can be described by a trend line.

2. Fit the trend line and extrapolate it.
3. Reverse the transformation to find a forecast value.

For instance, the data shown in Fig. 6–15 produce a trend line with a slope of 100 when transformed by squaring. The next value of the trend line through the transformed values is 500. To forecast the next value of X, the reverse transformation must be applied to 500. This reverse transformation is just taking the square root. The square root of 500 is about 22.4, and that value is therefore our forecast.

S-curves

Many business and economic factors rise at an accelerated rate for a time, and then continue to rise, but at a progressively slower rate, until some ceiling is reached. This pattern is typical of new product sales. If the product is successful, the first phase is characterized by ratio or exponential growth; the second phase is characterized by more gradual growth toward the ceiling, in this case the ultimate share of the market. If an estimate of this share-of-market can be made, and an estimate of the rate of growth in either the beginning or the central phase can be found, then some standard models can be used to forecast sales at each time period.

This is especially useful for forecasting the future growth of a product shortly after it has been introduced. The initial sales figures provide estimates of the growth rate at the beginning; the size of the market and an estimate of the final market share provide the ceiling.

A number of S-shaped curves has been analyzed and can provide useful formulas for this work. One of the more common ones is the Gompertz curve, which is a double-exponential. The formula is:

$$Y = A*B^{C^T}, \quad \text{where} \quad B > 1 \quad \text{and} \quad 0 < C < 1.$$

The initial value is $A*B$ at time 0, and A is the ceiling value. These parameters can be found for existing data by taking the logarithm twice, fitting a straight line to the results, and then taking the antilogarithms twice. Standard texts on economic forecasting provide details on fitting and using this curve and others. The important fact to keep in mind is that the curve is a model of a process, and that it must be an appropriate model if the results of the computations are to be meaningful.

PART 4 | THE USES OF UNCERTAINTY

CHAPTER 7

FORECASTING MAXIMUM VALUES

When a wholesaler is deciding how much stock he should buy to fill customer orders in the next month, he is really asking a fairly complex question. The question could be phrased as, "What is the maximum amount of this particular item that my customers are likely to request in the next month?" He does not aim to maintain enough stock to fill every conceivable volume of orders, because that would be prohibitively expensive. But he does want to have enough on hand to cover all the orders he really expects to get, so he can maximize profits by filling the greatest number of orders without either overstocks or backorders.

Looking at this as a forecasting question, the wholesaler is interested in forecasting the *maximum reasonable demand* for items he stocks. This is quite a different matter from the question dealt with in previous chapters. Exponential smoothing and seasonality analysis are methods of forecasting the most likely value of some factor, not the maximum. They give a central forecast value, and the forecaster can make his own guess about how far on either side of this forecast the actual values will fall. This approach can be very useful in certain situations, but it doesn't answer the wholesaler's real question at all.

Wholesalers aren't the only ones who have this kind of question, either. In building a dam, you need to forecast the maximum height of flood waters; an average will be no comfort when the waters spill over. In bridge building, you need the maximum weight of traffic; in school planning, the maximum likely number of students, and so on.

These questions are of interest in almost any situation in which increased capacity is associated with increased cost. You could build your dam a mile high to take care of the chance of a truly extraordinary flood, but, like the wholesaler with his overstocks, that would cost far more than it would be worth. Factory production facilities, urban transport systems, state welfare services, and dozens of other situations can all provide examples.

This chapter provides simple and useful methods of forecasting maximum reasonable values. The first method combines the expected or central-value forecasting discussed in previous chapters with use of facts about variability and errors. Then a variation for sales forecasting is discussed, and a model for use with infrequent occurrences, such as natural disasters or sales of an obsolete product, is also explained. These forecast models deal with one single factor; combinations of factors, including maximum likely totals, are discussed in Chapter 8.

THE BASIC IDEA

The first step in answering the question, "What is the maximum reasonable value of this factor in the next time period?" is to move away from the relatively vague phrase "maximum reasonable value" to a numerical representation. Typically, the question is rephrased in terms of percentage, as in, "What value has a 10% chance of being exceeded?" The particular percentage chosen may be 20%, 5%, 1%, or whatever else seems appropriate to the forecaster or his client.

In any case, he now views the question on a numerical basis. It can be pictured as it is in Fig. 7–1, as the search for a certain level which has been exceeded only rarely. As just indicated, "rarely" refers to a preselected percentage of actual cases. The forecaster simply counts the number of extreme cases, starting at the highest (or lowest) value, and notes the level at which his cumulative total equals his chosen percentage of the whole.

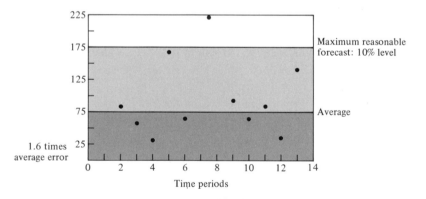

Fig. 7–1 Maximum reasonable forecast viewed as a level which is exceeded a small percentage of the time. The specific level depends on the percentage chosen.

The same basic idea can be applied to trending, seasonal, and curved models. For instance, Fig. 7–2 shows a typical maximum likely value line for a trending item. Actually, the model value changes as new data are obtained, so in practice the upper limit changes as shown in Fig. 7–3. In

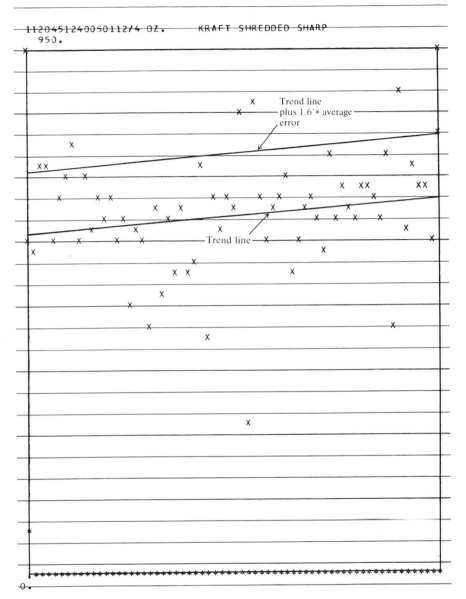

1120451240050112/4 OZ.   KRAFT SHREDDED SHARP
950.

Fig. 7–2 Overall trend line and maximum expectation line at 10% level. Compare with Fig. 7–3, which uses smoothed value instead of an overall trend line. There is a 10% chance that the next value will be above the upper line.

both cases, the maximum likely value line is found by adding a calculated amount to the central model value.

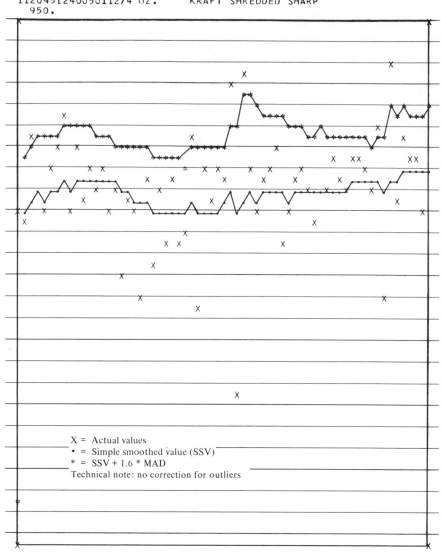

X = Actual values
• = Simple smoothed value (SSV)
* = SSV + 1.6 * MAD
Technical note: no correction for outliers

Fig. 7–3 Maximum likely value line for a slowly trending value, calculated at the 10% level. Only 10% of values will be above the calculated upper line. As new data are received, the model value and the estimate of variability (MAD, see text) are both updated—causing the upper line to change level.

The key to actually calculating the maximum likely value lies in finding the proper amount to add. This can be done by keeping track of forecast errors. It is easy to calculate the average error of the fitted model in the past, whether that model is a horizontal line, a trend line, a seasonal curve, or anything else. Extensive experience in statistics tells us that on the average 10% of the values of a randomly varying factor will be more than 1.6 times the average error above the central forecast value. Five percent of the time there will be values more than 2.05 times the average error above the central value, and .5% of the errors will be more than 3.2 times the average error above the central value. The odds for all other relative error values have been figured, too, and are available in tables; but these are the ones most commonly used.

The way to find a maximum reasonable forecast value, therefore, is as follows:

1. Specify "reasonable" as a numerical probability that the value will be exceeded, say, a 5% or 10% chance.

2. Measure past errors of the forecasting model. These errors are the forecast value subtracted from the actual value subsequently observed. The sign, indicating whether the error is positive or negative, is omitted from the calculation, so that negative and positive errors do not cancel out.

3. Find the error factor corresponding to your chosen probability. For example, as indicated above, a 10% probability corresponds to a factor of 1.6 times the average error, and a 5% probability corresponds to a factor of 2.05 times the average error.

4. Find the forecast of the maximum reasonable value by adding together the forecast of the central value for the next time period and the average error multiplied by the appropriate factor.

Exercise 1. Is the high variability of the upper limit in Fig. 7–3 a disadvantage? Would a smaller smoothing constant help? After a high value is observed, don't the factors level, trend, and error all increase? Does that have an effect on the variability of (the estimate of) the upper limit? What happens after a low actual value?

Exercise 2. Isn't the average variability related to the size of the forecast central value? Don't models with large values have proportionately larger errors? Doesn't this mean that for a trend or seasonal model the errors increase as the forecast increases? Shouldn't the maximum reasonable value reflect this by moving away from the model as values increase, as suggested in Fig. 7–4? Why or why not? The answer is in Chapter 8.

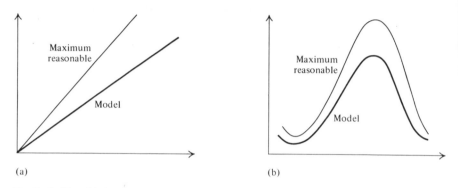

(a)   (b)

Fig. 7–4 Should the maximum reasonable value move further away from larger central values?

Mean Absolute Deviation (MAD)

The amount of variability in data is often measured by the standard deviation, which is a common statistical measure. It is equal to the square root of the sum of the squared deviations of the data from their average.

In forecasting, an analogous but different value is often more convenient. This is the Mean Absolute Deviation, or MAD. It is defined as the average of the absolute forecast errors; absolute means that the negative signs are discarded, leaving only positive error values. References above to the "average error" are intended to mean the MAD, and this name will be used from this point on. Some further discussion of MAD appears later, in connection with normal curves.

OUTLIERS AND OTHER ANOMALIES

The basic idea of forecasting maximum reasonable values is quite simple, but a good deal of care must be taken in applying it. One of the most common problems in using the concept involves unusually high or low values which happen for some nonrecurring reason. They are called *outliers*.

One of the exercises in an earlier chapter referred to the case of the tractor manufacturer who receives an order for six normal years' production from the government of Ruritania.   The question was whether the sales figure for the month in which this huge order is received should be used in forecasting.   The answer should obviously be no, because in normal operation nothing corresponding to the huge United Nations grant for tractors is ever likely to happen again.   In the statistician's manner of speaking, the Ruritanian order comes from a different *universe of discourse* from that which the forecasting system is intended to deal with.

What would happen if we did uncritically include this large figure in our normal forecasting system?   To begin with, the extremely large forecast error for that month would introduce a very large increase in level and trend.   This would distort future forecasts, magnifying them far above what they should be.   Although the harm would gradually be undone by the updating procedures in the succeeding normal months, there would still be a period of useless over-estimations of tractor sales.

Worse, from the point of view of this chapter, the MAD or uncertainty factor would be magnified.   The MAD, of course, is just the average of all past forecast errors, and allowing inclusion of the Ruritanian sale would introduce a very large error into the list.   This would mean that the maximum reasonable value, based on the average error, would be inflated.

The manufacturer probably wants to know the maximum reasonable sale in future months so he can produce enough tractors to fill all his orders in all but the few unusually high months.   He may specify the ninetieth percentile as the maximum-reasonable level, and then proceed to calculate this level by the forecast-plus-MAD procedure.   However, since the uncertainty estimate is now inflated, he will get an estimated maximum sale far above the true figure.   He will then produce more tractors than he can sell, expending money for materials and personnel to produce them, and may very well go out of business as a result.

Identifying and Dealing with Outliers

The definition suggested above is that any value which is not a guide to future values should be considered an outlier, and should be ignored in forecasting calculations.   Identifying outliers can be done by using the same basic idea used for finding the maximum reasonable demand: forecast the average and add on a factor reflecting uncertainty.   But for outliers we want to find a multiple of the MAD which corresponds to an *unreasonable* variation.   Statisticians have shown that there is a chance of less than 1% of exceeding the average plus 4 MADs, and so that is the commonly used threshold for outliers. Any value under this threshold is used in updating the forecast equations; any value over it is ignored.

Exercise 1. Estimate the outlier threshold for the item used in Figs. 7–2 and 7–3, using 4 MADs as the basis.

It should be noted that simply not updating the model when an outlier is encountered can lead to minor errors if a model more complex than the horizontal (average-value) model is used. This is because the value of the model itself needs to be updated in order to reflect the passage of time. If a trend model is used, and an outlier is encountered during updating, the values A1(T − 1) and A2(T − 1) must still be updated. The slope may not change, but on the basis of past experience the level still increases. The following formulas reflect these changes:

$$A1(T) = A1(T - 1) + A2(T - 1),$$
$$A2(T) = A2(T - 1).$$

Exercise 2. Choose values for level, trend, and MAD which reflect your business. For most, the trend will be about 10% of the level and the MAD will be about 1/4 of the level. Assume that a value equal to the outlier level is encountered (i.e., the level plus 4∗MAD), and go through the updating procedure for A1 and A2 using this value. How much error is introduced into (1) and forecast of the central value and (2) the forecast maximum reasonable value?

Using an outlier can distort the MAD as well as the smoothed value—and that can lead to fluctuations in your estimate of maximum values. Figure 7–5 shows how recognition of outliers can reduce this problem.

Initial Estimates

It is important to keep outliers in mind when thinking about the initial estimates of level, trend, and seasonal factors. There is a natural temptation for statisticians, because of long-followed habits, to simply calculate level, trend, and other factors by using the standard statistical formulas. But with computer methods available, the more accurate simulation approach can be used. This amounts to taking a very rough estimate of the model parameters (level, trend, or other factors) at the beginning of available data and going through the updating process for successive data points. Outliers can be identified and handled correctly in this process, instead of simply being buried among other data as they can be in the older statistical approach. The same applies to the pattern changes discussed in the next chapter.

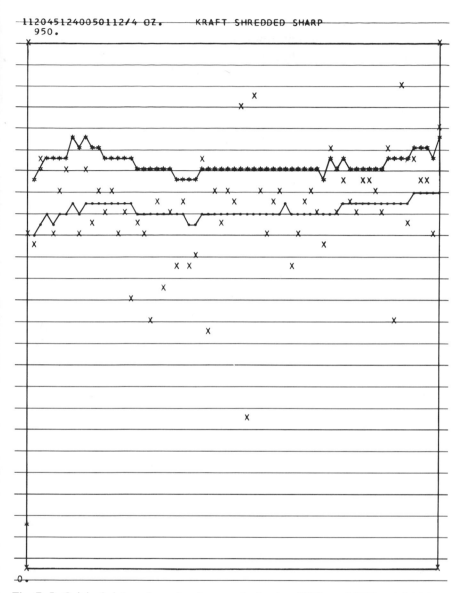

Fig. 7–5 Original data values, simple smoothed value (SSV), and SSV + 1.6∗MAD. Ten percent of data values should fall above the higher line. This graph was made using a demand filter that rejected outlying data values more than three MADs away from the SSV—compare with Fig. 7–3, which does not.

Both maximum reasonable forecasts and outliers are often pictured by using a normal curve. Figure 7–6 shows the frequency of different size sales for two items. One of them is purchased at a steady rate, so the variability is low; this is reflected in a narrow distribution. The other is quite variable, and has a spread-out distribution.

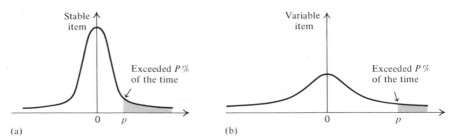

Fig. 7–6 Normal curves of forecast errors for relatively stable and relatively variable data. (a) Stable item. (b) Variable item.

As indicated in the diagrams, the value which is exceeded P% of the time depends on the variability. This variability can be measured by the MAD, or by the common statistical measure called the standard deviation. For a normal curve, the standard deviation is 1.25 times the MAD; it is defined as the square root of the average squared error. Squaring takes care of negative values by converting them to positive ones; in working with the MAD the sign is simply dropped.

The normal-curve view of error levels is helpful, but it should be kept in mind that the graph is a distribution of *forecast errors* rather than of actual data values. The "zero" value in the normal distribution is the forecast central value—the model value, not the actual zero. It is the forecast errors which are normally distributed, not the actual values. This is reflected in the other graphs shown in this chapter by the fact that the maximum reasonable level is a line that parallels the forecast or model line a given number of MADs above it, rather than being a horizontal level. Inattention to this point does not lead to conceptual errors but does lead to incorrect computer programs.

A VARIATION FOR FORECASTING SALES

It is relatively easy, both conceptually and practically, to establish a trend line and variability estimate for a time series. These can then be extrapolated to form forecasts of maximum likely values or confidence bands which denote both maximum and minimum reasonable expectations projected into the future. However, the simple trend line and variability measure model is not quite as realistic for sales data as it might be. For instance:

1. Sales usually grow or decline as a percentage of the previous values rather than by a fixed amount each period.

2. It is unrealistic to allow negative values for sales, as the simple model does.

3. The uncertainty estimate with the simple trend model is not related to the actual level, so that even if sales quadruple, the same estimate of variability is used. This is obviously inappropriate; the variability estimate should increase when the level increases.

One solution is to apply the above concept of central trend line and variability estimates, not to the actual values, but to the logarithms of successive values.

Figure 7–7 shows the difference between the forecasts based on these two alternate models. The trend line model, which suffers from the three defects described above, can be pictured by the first graph (a). The ratio model, which avoids all three, is shown in the second graph (b). In both cases, the factor being examined is increasing. If these figures represented sales, we might be dealing with a new and successfully introduced product. As you can see, the confidence band for the trend model does not grow wider as a higher level is reached, while the confidence level band for the ratio model does. This is natural and makes the ratio model a somewhat better picture.

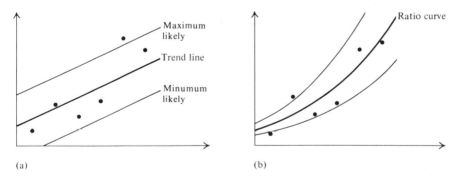

(a)   (b)

Fig. 7–7 Increasing sales. (a) Trend line and trend confidence band. (b) Ratio curve and confidence band.

Figure 7–8 shows the trend lines and ratio models for a factor which is decreasing. This might be monthly sales of an obsolete product. As the graphs show, the trend line model in this case produces negative expectations, while the ratio model does not. Furthermore, the ratio model "tails off" in a realistic manner, while the trend model plunges down to zero, and then below. Once again, the ratio model seems more appropriate.

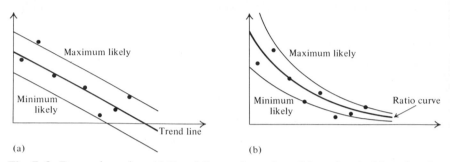

(a)   (b)

Fig. 7–8 Decreasing sales. (a) Trend line and trend confidence band. Note that the minimum falls below zero. (b) Ratio curve and confidence band.

Statistical Details: The Lognormal Distribution

Does statistical calculation of the simple trend line with variability estimate become excessively complex when the more sophisticated ratio model is used? No; in fact, the system becomes simpler to deal with. The trick lies in assuming that the actual values of sales are chosen from a random distribution around the central value which does not include any negative values, and is of the type called "lognormal." If this slightly more sophisticated assumption is made, the three problems listed above disappear. Somewhat more arithmetic is involved, but that can be handled by a computer without the forecaster even being aware of it.

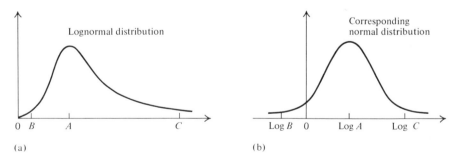

(a)   (b)

Fig. 7–9 Lognormal distribution. A is the most probable value.

A lognormal distribution is sketched in Fig 7–9, together with its corresponding normal distribution. The name *lognormal* means that the logarithms of the data values are distributed normally; the logarithms form a symmetrical pattern to which all the usual methods of finding maximum and minimum values by multiples of the MAD can be applied. The results can then be translated back to the values in the real lognormal distribution by reversing the transformation. The reverse is the exponential function e^x, or $\exp(x)$.

The lognormal population accurately represents actual experience with sales figures because (1) it contains no negative values, (2) there are a few very high values, and (3) the safety factor increases when the values increase. It also has the very interesting property—which the usual normal curve does not—that it represents processes where effects multiply. A normal curve represents total errors where small errors add up and sometimes cancel out, as in counting the number of heads in ten tosses of a coin. But addition in the normal curve corresponds to multiplication in the lognormal. The fact that the lognormal curve represents sales data so well therefore suggests that marketing effects multiply when paired rather than simply adding up.

Pursuit of this idea has led to a good deal of investigation of sales data and lognormal curves. The main result is the discovery that a distribution of the *number of items* falling in each dollar-volume class is lognormal.*
The evidence that actual monthly or weekly sales of a given item are lognormal is less clear, but the advantages of the lognormal over the normal curve cited above are sufficient to justify its use.

Figures 7–10, 7–11, and 7–12 show the result of forecasting with the lognormal model and two different confidence limits. The problem here is forecasting school enrollments, or survivals, so called because the statistical method called *cohort survival* is used. The cohort was originally a division of the Roman legion; it now means a group of any kind, but the name lends an air of romance to the procedure.

The Cohort Survival Method

The general idea is that, out of a given starting population, a certain percentage will remain in each succeeding year. Some members will leave or drop back (or in a Roman cohort, literally fail to survive), decreasing the percentage. The ranks may also be increased, by additions from outside; in that case, the percentage is more than one hundred. The forecasting procedure computes the appropriate percentage, or ratio, and applies it to the

---

* See, for instance, Brown, R. G., *Statistical Forecasting for Inventory Control*, McGraw-Hill, New York, 1959, and *Decision Rules for Inventory Management*, Holt, Rinehart, and Winston, New York, 1967.

```
WKB2        15:41     V    WED 03/26/69

ENROLLMENT FORECASTING

                    BEGINNING YEAR AND NUMBER OF YEARS --
? 1964,5


BIRTHS (-6YR) AND ENROLLMENTS 1 TO 12


    1964
? 419,575,552,465,429,413,455,392,319,312,316,273,247


    1965
? 431,600,543,536,490,445,435,458,411,309,334,262,261


    1966
? 436,655,550,544,532,503,457,465,471,383,327,292,244


    1967
? 439,688,617,531,551,542,521,473,468,439,413,271,263


    1968
? 445,651,615,528,504,528,517,497,456,444,435,382,263


LOGS OF SURVIVALS
    .4 -.1 -.0  .1  .0  .1  .0  .0 -.0  .1 -.2 -.0
    .4 -.1  .0 -.0  .0  .0  .1  .0 -.1  .1 -.1 -.1
    .5 -.1 -.0  .0  .0  .0  .0  .0 -.1  .1 -.2 -.1
    .4 -.1 -.2 -.1 -.0 -.0 -.0 -.0 -.1 -.0 -.1 -.0

AVERAGE SURVIVALS (LOGS)
    .4 -.1 -.1  .0  .0  .0  .0  .0 -.1  .0 -.1 -.1

VARIANCE OF LOGS OF SURVIVALS
    .0  .0  .0  .0  .0  .0  .0  .0  .0  .0  .0  .0


SURVIVALS
    143.2  94.4   97.1 105.4 103.7 105.3 100.7 104.8   96.9 107.1   82.9   95.6
    152.0  91.7  100.2  99.3 102.7 102.7 106.9 102.8   93.2 105.8   87.4   93.1
    157.8  94.2   96.5 101.3 101.9 103.6 103.5 100.6   93.2 107.8   82.9   90.1
    148.3  89.4   85.6  94.9  95.8  95.4  95.4  96.4   94.9  99.1   92.5   97.0


AVERAGE SURVIVAL
    150.2  92.4   94.7 100.1 101.0 101.7 101.5 101.1   94.5 104.9   86.3   93.9
```

Fig. 7–10 Setting up cohort survival forecast for school enrollments.

beginning value in order to predict the population in any given succeeding period.

   The beginning value must be supplied by the forecaster, and the figures here illustrate a neat mechanical feature as well as the forecasting method itself. The program used to forecast school enrollments was written for use on a timesharing terminal. These on-line, or interactive, terminals are designed to carry on a dialogue with the user, and can request data as required by the program. In this case such a request is indicated by a question mark, and the forecaster supplies the beginning population (in this case, the number of births six years before the present, which has proven to be more related to first-grade populations than kindergarten enrollments are), the beginning year and number of years, actual enrollment figures, and the confidence level he desires in his forecasts.

```
CONFIDENCE (PERCENT, MULTIPLE OF 5 . GE. 50)
? 95
NO. YEARS FORECAST
? 3


BIRTHS IN      1964
? 386


FORECAST, ENROLLMENTS AND RANGE    1969
CONFIDENCE LEVEL      95 PERCENT
```

GRADE	EXPECTED	MINIMUM	MAXIMUM
1	580.	541.	622.
2	411.	394.	430.
3	616.	548.	693.
4	616.	572.	663.
5	533.	502.	566.
6	512.	476.	552.
7	536.	494.	582.
8	523.	492.	556.
9	470.	455.	485.
10	478.	448.	511.
11	383.	351.	419.
12	409.	386.	432.

```
TOTAL ENROLLMENT    6067.7488
```

Fig. 7–11 Results with 95 % confidence level.

The computer program measured the variability of the survival ratios from year to year as part of the process of finding the average ratio. This variability was also used to provide confidence levels: the user could specify any level of confidence he desired and the program would compute the width of the corresponding band.

```
1 TO LOOP, 2 TO END
? 1

CONFIDENCE (PERCENT, MULTIPLE OF 5 .GE. 50)
? 50
NO. YEARS FORECAST
? 1


BIRTHS IN       1964
? 386


FORECAST, ENROLLMENTS AND RANGE     1969
CONFIDENCE LEVEL       50 PERCENT


    GRADE      EXPECTED        MINIMUM     MAXIMUM

      1          580.            566.        594.

      2          411.            405.        417.

      3          616.            592.        642.

      4          616.            600.        632.

      5          533.            522.        544.


USED      43.67 UNITS.
BYE

*** OFF AT 15:58    ELAPSED TERMINAL TIME =    18 MIN.
```

Fig. 7–12 Results of a trial with 50% confidence level. Note that the range between maximum and minimum likely values is narrower than in Fig. 7–11.

To be quite certain that the forecast covers most possibilities, the band must be quite wide. This is reflected in the values shown for the 95% confidence limit, which produces a wide forecast band. The 50% value produces a narrower forecast band, but, of course, there is only a 50% chance that the actual values will be within the limits shown. In fact, if the model is correct, the enrollment should be within the calculated limits half the time, and outside them the other half.

This program has been used successfully to forecast enrollments for a number of suburban school districts, and incidentally turned up an interesting fact. In gathering and analyzing the data required by the program, someone noticed that the seventh-grade enrollments showed a consistently larger increase than those of previous grades. The implication seems to be that upwardly-mobile parents tend to move from the city to the suburbs, where there are "better" schools, the year that their children enter junior high school and begin preparing for college.

Exercise. Do you think that the band corresponding to a given confidence level should expand (grow wider) as projections are made further into the future (e.g., one year ahead, then two years, three, etc.)? If you don't think so, then do you think you can forecast ten years ahead as accurately as you can one year ahead? If you do think so, then do you think that the model you are using will have an increasing MAD as time passes? Does a linear (trend) model provide increasing width as the distance ahead of the forecast increases? What about the cohort survival method?

DESCRIBING INFREQUENT OCCURRENCES

The methods described above for finding maximum likely values, based on an estimate of the most likely value and the size of the error distribution, are obviously most useful when applied to data which contain few zeroes. They are rather hard to apply to time series like the following:

$$0, 0, 0, 1, 0, 1, 0, 0, 0.$$

Exercise. Find the average and the Mean Absolute Deviation (MAD) for this series, and use them to estimate the maximum reasonable expectation for the series. Is the result reasonable? Why or why not?

In dealing with a sequence of large numbers, we can use the device of choosing a percentage level or a few percentage levels. Then we can ask what value has that chance of being exceeded. This method is not aimed at finding the precise probability that a given value will occur, but only at finding a reasonable outside limit.

In the case of a series of very small numbers containing many zeroes, a more discrete approach is more convenient. Instead of asking what value will be exceeded 10% of the time, we turn the question around and ask what the chance is that there will be any (i.e., more than zero) occurrences, more than one, more than two, and so on. The values in this time series might be sales of a high-priced, low-volume item; they might be uses of a major spare part, such as a replacement diesel engine in a transportation operation; they might be occurrences of emergencies such as earthquakes, nuclear attacks, or calls for ambulance service. The range of subjects which involve infrequent occurrences of an important event is quite as broad as the range of activities which involve random deviations of large numbers of events.

The easiest way to visualize these low frequency occurrences is to choose a time period in which your event has a low but not zero chance of occurrence. For instance, in sales of heavy equipment at a branch office the period might be a month; for arrival of telephone orders at a stationery supply firm the interval might be an hour. Historical records can be used to tabulate the number of periods when there are no occurrences, the number of times there is one, the number of times there are two, and so on. The tabulations are easy to display as bar charts like that shown in Fig. 7–13. The tabulations are also often converted to percentages or probabilities for easier comparison.

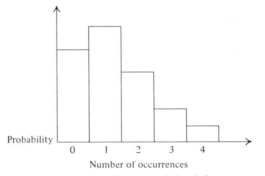

Fig. 7–13 Typical Poisson distribution describing infrequent occurrences.

Making It Easy

Mathematical study of bar charts like these has shown that without going through the trouble of actually collecting, tabulating, and averaging historical frequencies it is still very easy to estimate the probability that there will be more than any given number of occurrences in a particular time period. All you need to know is the total number of occurrences over a relatively long period of time (say, 100 times the basic measurement interval). Then the average number of occurrences in the basic interval can be found easily; you just divide by 100. Call the average A. The following formula gives the probability of zero, 1, 2, or N occurrences in any interval:

$$PROB(K) = e^{-A}*A^{K}/K!$$

The negative exponent with e indicates division; $e^{-A} = 1/e^{A}$. And the exclamation point after K in "K!" denotes the product of the first K integers: $K! = 1*2*3*\cdots*K$. This product is called "K factorial." The value of e is about 2.8.

This Poisson model is useful for a number of common problems, such as that of stocking spare parts. A truck fleet maintained a stock of spare diesel engines which could be installed in the trucks as breakdowns occurred. The out-of-service engines were sent off for repair before being placed in the inventory of spare engines; the firm needed to deal with the question, "How many spares should we have?"

There were relatively few breakdowns, and they occurred at random. The occurrence of breakdowns was thus a Poisson process. Various occurrence rates were investigated. The probability of different numbers of breakdowns in a month, for a hypothetical but typical number of breakdowns, is as follows: Suppose there are 100 diesel engines in use and 10 in reserve. Suppose that it takes six months to get one repaired, on the average, and that there is one breakdown per month serious enough to require repair. Let RD represent the repair duration: RD = 6 months. A simple multiplication shows that the average number of breakdowns in an RD period is 1∗6 = 6. That is, A = 6. Then the Poisson formula gives the following probabilities of breakdowns in a period of length RD:

$$PROB(0) = .0025$$

$$PROB(1) = .015$$

$$PROB(2) = .048$$

$$PROB(3) = .090$$

$$\vdots \qquad \vdots$$

$$PROB(10) = .0042$$

An Application in Operations Research

The objective of the work described in the case above was to determine how many spare engines should be kept. Knowing the distribution of breakdowns was some help in making the analysis, since it enabled forecasts of the maximum reasonable demand to be made. But this forecast was only the first step in the solution. The next step was to design a simple mathematical model of the repair process and then use it to determine how many spares should be kept. The analysis is described below.

Analyses of this type, which involve understanding the processes at work and then applying statistics or other mathematical concepts to find the "best way" are both common and important. This kind of work is called *operations research* or *management science*—and forecasting is one of its keystones. Computer modeling is another closely related subject.

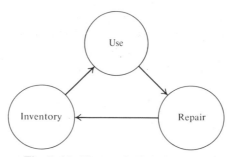

Fig. 7–14 The repaired engine cycle.

The diesel engine analysis was intended to find the minimum number of spares which would give any specified level of service, in terms of unfilled demands per year. It began with a diagram such as the one in Fig. 7–14.

As illustrated, the spare engines cycled from inventory to usage to repair shop and then back to inventory. This meant that replenishment of inventory depended on previous usages from inventory, since an issue from inventory corresponded to a breakdown of an engine being used, which was then sent for repair. One can attach numbers to the various parts of the diagram by observing that there is a certain number in use, a certain number being repaired, and a certain number in inventory at any given time. To give these names:

NU is the number in use.

NR is the number being repaired.

NI is the number in inventory.

NS is the total number in reserve, including those in inventory and those being repaired.
That is, NS = NR + NI.

If the simplifying assumption is made that the repair time is constant, then the number being repaired at a given time is simply the number of usages which have occurred in the past repair duration, RD. If breakdowns occur randomly among those items in use, then the distribution of the number being repaired at any time is given by the Poisson distribution of breakdowns in period RD.

As shown in Fig. 7–13, there is a certain probability that there will be no breakdowns, another probability that there will be one breakdown, a probability that there will be two breakdowns, and so on in the entire population of those items in use (NU) in a period of length RD. If the total number of breakdowns in some relatively long period (say, the last year) is known, then these probabilities are easy to calculate. The average number of breakdowns in an RD period is denoted AD; given AD, the probability of 0, 1, 2, . . . breakdowns in the period RD is given by the familiar Poisson formula

$$PROB(K) = e^{-AD} * AD^K / K.$$

There will be stockout whenever NR is larger than NS. But we have just provided a formula for the distribution of NR. We can, therefore, find out how often NR will be larger than NS. That is, we can predict the percentage of the time that there will be a stockout, by simply adding up the values PROB(K) for all K's larger than NS. Stated another way,

PROB OF STOCKOUT = PROB(NS + 1) + PROB(NS + 2) + · · · .

Fortunately, the values of sums like these are tabulated in statistical handbooks. For the hypothetical data given at the beginning of this example, RD = 6 and AD = 1. For these values, a statistical table shows that the probability of exceeding 10 in a period of length RD is 0.0413. So there is a 4.13% chance of a stockout at any given time, if there are 10 spares in all.

This probability can be combined with information about the usage rate to give the number of unfilled requests per year. This will be the annual usage times the probability of a stockout. In this example, there are 12 usages per year on the average, so there are 12*.0413 = .495 unfilled requests per year.

Maintaining a Service Level

The method described and illustrated above can also be used in conjunction with a service level. The service level needs to be stated in terms of the maximum acceptable number of unfilled demands per year. For instance, an essential spare part might be assigned an average of one request per year that cannot be filled from inventory. A more routine part might correspond to two unfilled requests per year, and a critical item to one unfilled request every two years. These numbers are cited as examples of stockout frequencies that might be appropriate; the actual specification of service level numbers is operating management's responsibility.

Once the service level numbers have been specified, however, this method will tell you the minimum number of spares that you need to achieve that level of service. Although it is more complex than the method given for estimating the maximum reasonable value of a factor which exhibits random variation about a model, it does the same thing for you. Both methods answer an instance of the question, "What is the maximum reasonable level to expect for this factor?"

CHAPTER 8

DETECTING CHANGES AND
COMBINING VARIABLES

The various forecasting methods described up to this point all depend on extrapolation. They all involve finding a model which describes the process you are interested in, fitting it to the data as closely as possible by calculating various parameters, updating them when possible, and then forecasting by simply extrapolating the fine-tuned model into the future.

In every case, the actual forecasting is done by simply projecting the best possible estimates of past events and past patterns into the future. This is fine so long as the pattern does not change. But in fact the pattern often does change. A product which is not popular today and has not been popular for 20 years may suddenly become stylish. Sales may begin to pick up; yet if forecasting is done on the basis of the past only, the forecasts will be wrong.

There is not much that can be done about anticipating such changes. But we can guard against their effects by making sure they are recognized as soon as possible. Once the pattern has changed and the old forecasting method in use is no longer appropriate, statistical techniques can be used to ensure that the inappropriate forecasting data are used as little as possible.

The problem of recognizing real changes is more complex than may at first appear, because there are typically random errors of various sizes in a forecasting system. Errors are always with us; the actual effect of a change in pattern is simply to increase the errors. Yet the errors fluctuate on their own. How does one determine when an error is the result of chance random fluctuations and when it is the result of change in the underlying pattern?

THE BASIC IDEA

Figure 8–1 shows a graph of monthly usages of an industrial part. Inspection of the actual values shows what appear to be three distinct periods, with different usage patterns in each. From month 1 to month 8, usage is stable at a medium level. Then it climbs steeply upward to a higher but much more variable level, from which it falls at month 18. Then there is a period of trending usage at a low level until the end of the data at month 27.

13657EA 25CLUSTER POWER VF 0009753 HAULPAK

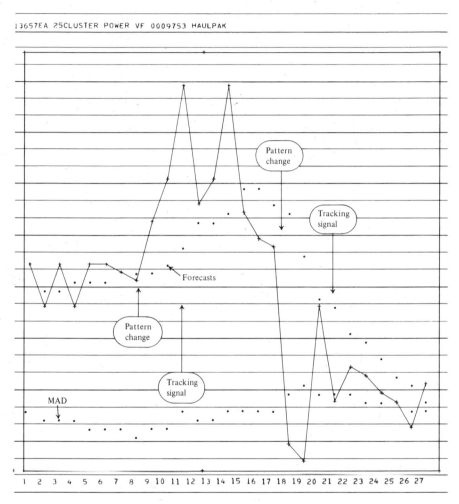

Fig. 8–1 Example of a time series containing pattern changes. When the pattern changes, a new model should be used. The change is recognized by observing the increase in error size by means of a tracking signal.

If reasonably accurate forecasting is to be done in this situation, the appropriate model should be in use for each of these three periods. Suppose the correct model is in use for the first phase, and then something changes in the real world so that the usage pattern changes as at T8. Then the forecasts made on the basis of the first model will be grossly erroneous. In fact, as is apparent in the graph, the errors for T9, T10, T11, and T12 are all very large compared to previous errors. And they are all positive errors—the model in use systematically underestimates the real values. If the forecasts were inaccurate but some were high and some were low, as in T1 to T8, we could conclude that the model was all right but that the item was highly variable. In phase two, from T9 on, this is not the case.

A numerical measure of the inappropriateness of the model can be based on these observations. You can simply add up all the errors. If the model "goes down the middle," some errors will be positive and some will be negative; the total will be close to zero because of canceling. But if the model is highly inappropriate, the total error will be large on either the positive or the negative side.

Tracking Signals and Thresholds

Similarly, if successive errors are smoothed together, a value very much above or below zero will indicate inappropriateness. The smoothed value, after all, is simply a weighted sum. For several reasons, it is usually more convenient to use the smoothed error than the total error. The smoothed error is therefore the basic building block in the general system for recognizing changes in data patterns.

When the smoothed error exceeds a predetermined threshold level, we conclude that a pattern change has occurred, and we say that a *tracking signal* has been tripped. This terminology stems from the fact that the smoothed error, or rather a modification of the smoothed error, tracks the level of the error in the system. It signals us when the level of error becomes too high.

But what is the threshold level, and how do we set it? We want the signal to tell us when the smoothed error, indicating the overall error level, is too big. What does "too big" really mean?

The answer can be found by considering the random variation in the data, as reflected by the MAD. There is some chance that two or three data values in a row will be high or low; their actual deviations from zero are distributed according to the normal law. So it should be possible to calculate a 90% level for the smoothed error based on the distribution of errors. The result will be a significance test just like that used in testing correlations and trends.

The mathematical argument for this procedure will be given later, and more statistical details can be found in another book by R. G. Brown.*

---

* Brown, R. G., *Statistical Forecasting for Inventory Control,* McGraw-Hill, New York, 1959, Chapter 2.

A variety of difficulties arise in trying to apply the statistical theory, however. For instance, successive errors are often related. A high value is often followed by another high value, an autocorrelation measured by the correlation of X(T) and X(T − 1). If error patterns are not truly random, the 90% level of the weighted sum of successive errors will actually be somewhat different from the theoretical result.

Experienced forecasters are well aware of this. In practice, a threshold is usually best set using trial and error. A typical value is 0.55∗MAD, although values from 0.5 to 0.7 are encountered in practice

In summary, the steps used to determine if the data pattern has changed are:

1. Establish a tracking signal threshold, usually about 0.5∗MAD.

2. Calculate the smoothed error.

3. Every time the smoothed error is updated, compare its absolute value with the threshold. If the SE exceeds the threshold, the pattern has probably changed.

It should be noted that all three steps are easy for a computer to do.

Does It Work?

As indicated on the graph shown in Fig. 8–1, tracking signals for the data shown appeared at time 11 and at time 21. Based on hindsight, it appears that basic pattern changes occurred at times 8 and 16. The tracking signal certainly recognized the pattern changes; the delays were 3 and 5 periods, respectively. The calculations are displayed in Fig. 8–2.

Of course, the ultimate criterion of whether a forecasting tool like the tracking signal works is whether it produces better forecasts. That is, the test is whether the errors are smaller. In fact, the use of tracking signals does reduce the error as reflected in MAD. Of course, the simple fact of recognizing inappropriate models doesn't do this by itself; what reduces the error is the change made in response to the appearance of a tracking signal. The tracking signal just enables you to make appropriate changes sooner than you otherwise would recognize the need. And in the case of large masses of data, such as records of large inventories, the tracking signal will point out changes that would otherwise be conveniently left buried in detailed status reports. A picture like Fig. 8–5 on p. 168 will help you tell whether a system does recognize changes effectively.

260313657EA 25CLUSTER POWER VF 0009753 HAULPAK			38.06	232.0	0031

55.0	44.0	56.0	45.0	55.0	56.0
54.0	50.0	67.0	80.0	105.0	72.0
80.0	106.0	71.0	62.0	60.0	7.0
2.0	44.0	18.0	28.0	25.0	21.0
17.0	11.0	23.0	0.0	0.0	0.0
0.0	0.0	0.0	0.0	0.0	0.0
0.0	0.0	0.0	0.0		

```
AVERAGE        52
INITIAL LEVEL AND TREND                        49.13      .77

SMOOTHING FACTORS FOR A1  A2  XMAD   .10    .05    .10
TRACKING SIGNAL THRESHOLD      .50
```

MO	ACT	XHAT	ERR	XMAD	SE	A1	A2	TRACK	H1	H2
2	44	50	-6	14	-1	49	.2	.04	.10	.05
3	56	49	7	13	0	50	.8	.01	.10	.05
4	45	51	-6	12	-0	50	.2	.04	.10	.05
5	55	51	4	11	0	51	.7	.00	.10	.05
6	56	52	4	11	0	52	.7	.04	.10	.05
7	54	53	1	10	1	53	.6	.05	.10	.05
8	50	53	-3	9	0	53	.3	.01	.10	.05
9	67	53	14	10	1	55	1.2	.15	.10	.05
10	80	56	24	11	4	58	1.8	.34	.10	.05
11	105	60	45	14	8	65	2.9	.55	.10	.05
TRACKING SIGNAL AT T		11								
12	72	68	4	13	0	68	-.5	.03	.18	.09
13	80	68	12	13	2	70	.3	.12	.16	.09
14	106	70	36	16	5	76	2.5	.32	.15	.09
15	71	78	-7	15	4	77	-.6	.26	.14	.08
16	62	76	-14	15	2	75	-1.3	.14	.13	.08
17	60	73	-13	15	0	72	-1.3	.03	.13	.08
18	7	70	-63	19	-6	63	-5.1	.30	.12	.07
19	2	57	-55	23	-11	51	-5.1	.47	.12	.07
20	44	46	-2	21	-10	46	-1.9	.48	.11	.07
21	18	44	-26	21	-12	41	-3.5	.54	.11	.07
TRACKING SIGNAL AT T		21								
22	28	37	-9	20	-1	36	-2.2	.05	.18	.09
23	25	33	-8	19	-2	32	-2.3	.09	.16	.09
24	21	30	-9	18	-2	28	-2.4	.13	.15	.09
25	17	26	-9	17	-3	25	-2.6	.18	.14	.08
26	11	22	-11	17	-4	21	-2.8	.24	.13	.08
27	23	18	5	15	-3	19	-1.7	.19	.13	.08

```
FINAL LEVEL AND TREND                      18.53     -1.70


XMAD   SMOOTHED ABS ERROR              15.36

SMOOTHED ERROR                        -2.99
```

Fig. 8–2 Example of tracking signal calculations. A1 and A2 are the calculated level and trend; TRACK is the ratio of the smoothed error (SE) to the MAD. When this ratio exceeds the threshold value of .50, a message is printed and the updating constants for level and trend are temporarily increased.

```
24 DJIA WEEKLY CLOSINGS BEGINNING 1 07 70
  802.0    787.0    782.0    759.0    754.0    757.0
  757.0    768.0    788.0    778.0    768.0    790.0
  792.0    790.0    776.0    747.0    734.0    717.0
  702.0    662.0    700.0    695.0    684.0    699.0
    0.0      0.0      0.0      0.0      0.0      0.0
    0.0      0.0      0.0      0.0      0.0      0.0
    0.0      0.0      0.0      0.0
```

AVERAGE	773							

INITIAL LEVEL AND TREND   808.20   -9.91

SMOOTHING FACTORS FOR A1   A2   XMAD   .10   .05   .10
TRACKING SIGNAL THRESHOLD   .50

MO	ACT	XHAT	ERR	XMAD	SE	A1	A2	TRACK	H1	H2
2	787	798	-11	26	11	797	-10.5	.44	.10	.05
3	782	787	-5	24	10	786	-10.7	.41	.10	.05
4	759	775	-16	23	7	774	-11.5	.31	.10	.05
5	754	762	-8	22	6	761	-12.0	.26	.10	.05
6	757	750	7	20	6	750	-11.6	.28	.10	.05
7	757	739	18	20	7	741	-10.7	.35	.10	.05
8	768	730	38	22	10	734	-8.8	.46	.10	.05
9	788	725	63	26	15	731	-5.6	.59	.10	.05

TRACKING SIGNAL AT T   9

MO	ACT	XHAT	ERR	XMAD	SE	A1	A2	TRACK	H1	H2
10	778	726	52	29	5	735	-.6	.18	.18	.09
11	768	734	34	29	8	740	2.4	.28	.16	.09
12	790	742	48	31	12	750	6.5	.39	.15	.09
13	792	756	36	32	14	761	9.5	.46	.14	.08
14	790	771	19	30	15	773	11.0	.49	.13	.08
15	776	784	-8	28	13	783	10.4	.45	.13	.08
16	747	794	-47	30	7	788	7.0	.22	.12	.07
17	734	795	-61	33	-0	788	2.6	.00	.12	.07
18	717	790	-73	37	-7	782	-2.5	.20	.11	.07
19	702	780	-78	41	-14	771	-7.7	.35	.11	.07
20	662	763	-101	47	-23	752	-14.4	.49	.11	.07
21	700	738	-38	46	-25	734	-16.8	.53	.11	.06

TRACKING SIGNAL AT T   21

MO	ACT	XHAT	ERR	XMAD	SE	A1	A2	TRACK	H1	H2
22	695	717	-22	44	-2	713	-18.9	.05	.18	.09
23	684	694	-10	40	-3	693	-19.8	.07	.16	.09
24	699	673	26	39	-0	677	-17.6	.00	.15	.09

FINAL LEVEL AND TREND   676.66   -17.55

XMAD SMOOTHED ABS ERROR   39.04

SMOOTHED ERROR   -.07

Fig. 8–3 Tracking signals for stock market values.

Another example is shown in Fig. 8–3. These are weekly DJIA values
to which a trend model has been applied. A tracking signal is reported when
the ratio SE/MAD is over 0.50 (that is, when the smoothed error is larger
than half the MAD). Figure 8–4 shows the resulting graph.

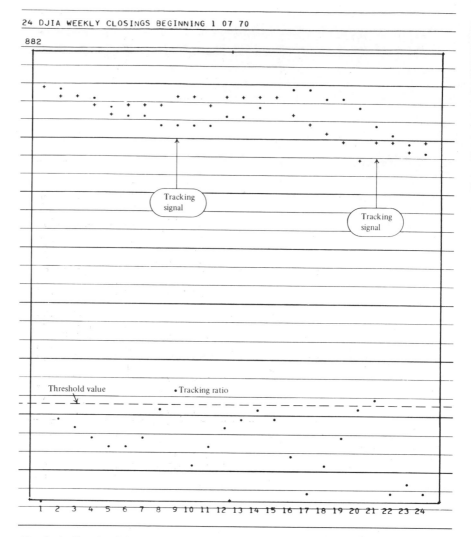

24 DJIA WEEKLY CLOSINGS BEGINNING 1 07 70

Fig. 8–4 Graph of the calculations shown in Fig. 8–3. Note that the tracking signals follow a string of over- or underestimates.

Responding to Tracking Signals

The tracking signal is a notification that a new model is needed. However, since the pattern is new, there is not much historical data to go on in finding the newly appropriate model. Two procedures should therefore be put into action:

1. Judgment should be applied by having persons familiar with the process review the data and indicate what kind of change has occurred and what the effects should be. For instance, if the data are for sales, the marketing manager may know that the particular product has found a new use or a new market, and he may be able to guess at the new sales level.

2. Rapid updating of the guess (or of the old parameters if no judgment is available) should be used, in order to make use of new data as quickly as possible.

In a computerized forecasting system, step one can and should be done by the computer. A report to management should be produced as soon as the computer program identifies an inappropriate forecast model, and the report should be routed to the man who can supply the most relevant judgment. The figures printed out in Fig. 8–3 are typical of such reports.

The rapid updating can be supplied in a variety of forms, but it should be programmed into the updating procedure. One common method is to simply use a larger set of smoothing constants for level, trend, or other parameters, for a fixed number of time periods after a tracking signal occurs. Fast updating for six months, for example, should take care of the kind of changes shown by the data in Fig. 8–1.

An alternative is to immediately raise the smoothing constant values, and then let them gradually decline towards the base values. This can be done easily by smoothing the constants in use together with the base values at each updating period. This is the approach followed in the calculations shown in Fig. 8–3, and it seems to work quite smoothly.

One other step needs to be taken when a tracking signal occurs: the smoothed error must be reset to zero. Otherwise the original tracking signal will probably be followed by a second one, which would only confuse people.

A NOTE ON TECHNICAL LEVEL

The next part of this chapter, up to the section labeled "Change of Time Period," is more technical than the rest of the book, in the sense that it tries to explain the mathematical reasoning that underlies the tracking signal concept. When a statistician is developing new or improved forecasting methods, he has in mind a model of the process to be forecast. This model involves several interleaved layers of normal curves, standard deviations, and combinations of these and other factors. The model itself is usually quite simple under these layers of detail, but that detail can confuse the uninitiated. And statistical texts usually concentrate on the detail, assuming that the reader already understands the basic model concepts. This makes it nearly impossible for the nonprofessional to read statistical texts.

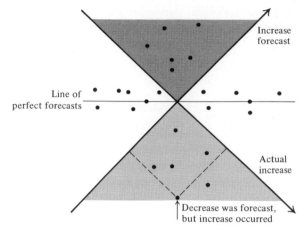

Fig. 8–5 This picture of forecast errors can help us tell whether a forecasting system recognizes changes efficiently. Any points which fall in the shaded areas are the result of turning point errors—forecast increases that turned out to be decreases, or vice versa. The Dutch economist Henri Theil makes extensive use of this type of picture in his *Applied Economic Forecasting* (Rand-McNally, 1966), where it is the basis of some sophisticated evaluation procedures useful in forecasting large-scale economic phenomena.

The rest of this chapter tries to explain some of the statistical concepts involved in developing forecasting procedures, for two reasons:

1. This slightly deeper level of mathematics will show the mathematically inclined reader a little bit more of what is going on behind the procedures explained elsewhere in the book, and give him a conceptual model he can refine or develop to fit his own needs.

2. The material will provide an introduction to the statistical analysis of time series for the student or system developer who wants to go further, and should make reading books like Brown's *Smoothing, Forecasting, and Prediction of Discrete Time Series** easier and more productive.

Obviously the reader who is not interested in mathematical statistics should not try to master the material, but should simply skim the rest of the chapter before going on to the final section of the book. Some of the

---

* Prentice-Hall, Englewood Cliffs, N.J., 1962.

material, however, especially the section on stock portfolios, will at least show him why other people bother with the details.

COMBINING VARIABLES

Many kinds of random variables are added together for a variety of purposes. In fact, most random variables can be regarded as the sum of a number of random components. The stock market averages, of course, are random variables which are obviously derived from the sum of individual stock prices, themselves random variables. Sales of a given consumer product on a given day are influenced by a wide range of random variables—the weather, promotional sales in progress in the selling store, sales in progress in other stores, delays and congestion in shopper transportation, the prosperity of buyers. And monthly sales of a product can be regarded as the sum of daily sales, so that the variable "monthly sales" can be studied as the total of a number of "daily sales" variables.

Errors in a forecasting system are also a normal random variable, and a tracking signal is a sum of forecast errors. Forecast errors are added up in calculating MAD, in calculating standard deviations, and in going from weekly data to monthly data or making other changes in time-scale. Understanding combinations of errors, then, is a fundamental aspect of forecasting, and the next several pages show one very useful technique for dealing with it.

The Basic Rule

The basic statistical fact which underlies calculation of variability for combinations of factors is:

The variability of the combination is the square root of the total of the individual squared variabilities, if the variability is measured by the standard deviation ($= 1.25*$MAD and if the factor is normally distributed).

For instance, if there are two products in a sales line, one with average sales of $100 per month and variability of $30 per month, and another with sales of $150 and a variability of $35, then the variability of total sales in that line is found as follows:

Variability of product 1, squared:	900
Variability of product 2, squared:	1225
Sum of squared variabilities:	2125
Square root of sum:	46

These calculations show that the net effect on variability of combining two factors is to produce *less than* complete addition of the individual factors' variabilities. This is because the upward and downward variations in the two factors often cancel each other out. When one is high, the other is likely to be low. Sometimes the two factors reinforce each other, so that unusually high (or low) data values from each population add together to produce an unusually high (or low) total. But in general, the variability of a combination is a *smaller percentage* of the combined average than the individual variabilities are of the individual averages. Of course, this general idea applies only when there is *no relationship* between the variables. That is, it works only when they are truly random and not correlated with each other. For instance, if high sales of item 1 tend to be associated with high sales of item 2, then the canceling effect would not hold to the same degree, and neither would the formula for combining variability. For this reason it is especially important to determine whether two factors which are being combined are associated before simply applying the formula.

Exercise. Sales for a given product have been recorded on a weekly basis. Management wants to know what variability it can expect in *monthly* sales figures. Regard each month's sales as the total of four weekly sales figures, and assume that there is no direct relationship among sales in adjacent weeks. That is, autocorrelation is zero. If the average weekly sale is 10 units and the weekly variability is 4 units, use the basic idea explained above to calculate the monthly variability. Test your answer by noting that 4 is 40% of the weekly sales; your answer should be less than 40% of the monthly sales.

Application to Tracking Signals

As already mentioned, the tracking signal is the sum of a series of forecast errors. These errors are randomly distributed, so the tracking signal can be viewed as the sum of a sequence of random variables. Then, if a measure of their variability is available, the variability of the total can be calculated by applying the basic rule. The variability, of course, can be measured: it is the MAD. It takes just one step of imagination to regard each of the errors as the representative of a population of errors with a variability of MAD. Then the smoothed error, basis of the tracking signal, is the weighted sum of a sequence of random variables which all have the same variability.

Once the rule for combining variability is applied, the result is a measure of the variability of the tracking ratio itself. If the forecast model is appropriate, the average value of the tracking signal will be zero. The MAD of the tracking signal will then reflect the chance of a high or low value occurring because of accidental variations alone. This MAD can be used to calculate the 10 % or 5 % or 1 % test value for the tracking signal. For instance, the 1 % value will be a number which is exceeded by the tracking signal only 1 % of the time, on the basis of the random variability in the error. If the tracking signal is above this test value, then, it is likely to be the result of an inappropriate model rather than pure random error.

The calculations below result in a general formula for estimating the MAD of the tracking signal, based on the MAD of the forecasting system as a whole. Although the smoothed-error tracking signal is most convenient in practice, the use of the combination rule is easier to illustrate for the average error. This is done below, and the one additional step needed to apply the rule to smoothed errors is explained. The reader can then carry out the analysis for smoothed errors as an exercise, or follow the discussion in one of the texts mentioned; the overall line of reasoning is the same.

The following steps involve some mathematical reasoning; they are a good example of the kind of work that a statistician does in developing a forecasting technique. The reasoning should be understandable to anyone who remembers the basic rule for combining variables, but it will probably take rereading for people not used to mathematical or statistical reasoning.

Statistical Analysis of the Average Error

From a statistical point of view the forecast errors produced by a good model will be a normal population with a mean of zero and a reasonably small standard deviation or MAD. This simply reflects the fact that a good model "goes right down the middle" of the actual values, with about the same number of positive errors as negative ones, and with more small errors than large ones. Figure 8–6 illustrates this ideal model. For a normal

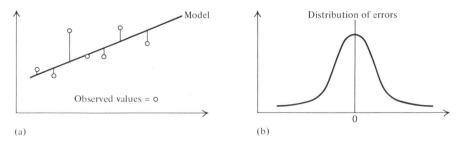

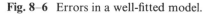

Fig. 8–6 Errors in a well-fitted model.

distribution the standard deviation (SD) is 1.25*MAD. The variance V is the square of the SD. And as the basic rule indicates, when values from two independent normal populations are added, the variances add.

Suppose we are interested in finding the variance of the sum of the errors in two forecasting periods. The error in each period is drawn from a normal population of errors which has a variance equal to the square of the standard deviation. If we denote the variance of the sum of the errors in the two periods by V2, then according to the basic rule,

$$V2 = 2*V.$$

If we are interested in averaging the two errors instead of just adding them, the values of the errors must be multiplied by $\frac{1}{2}$. The MAD of the halved errors is then $\frac{1}{2}$*MAD; the SD is 1.25*$\frac{1}{2}$*MAD; and V is (1.25*$\frac{1}{2}$*MAD)^2. The average error is the sum of these halved errors. The variance of the average can be denoted VA2, for variance/average error/two periods. Then:

$$VA2 = 2*(1.25*\tfrac{1}{2}*MAD)^2.$$

The standard deviation of the two-period average, SDA2, is just the square root of the variance:

$$SDA2 = SQRT(VA2)$$
$$= SQRT(2)*1.25*\tfrac{1}{2}*MAD.$$

The SQRT(2) and the $\frac{1}{2}$ can be canceled to give

$$SDA2 = 1.25*MAD/SQRT(2).$$

Finally, the MAD of the average of the two errors is just the standard deviation divided by 1.25:

$$MADA2 = (1.25*MAD/SQRT(2))/1.25$$
$$= MAD/SQRT(2).$$

This reasoning can be repeated for N periods instead of two periods. The steps could be written:

$$VAN = N*(1.25*1/N*MAD)^2,$$
$$SDAN = SQRT(VAN) = SQRT(N)*1.25*1/N*MAD,$$
$$SDAN = 1.25*MAD/SQRT(N),$$
$$MADAN = MAD/SQRT(N).$$

This shows that the average error in N time periods is MAD/SQRT(N), which is much smaller than the average one-period error, as we would expect from the existence of canceling. The important thing about this formula is that it gives us a way of calculating the variability of the average of any number of errors.

If we have been using a forecasting system for nine months, for example, we should have a pretty good estimate of the MAD. The average of the nine forecasting errors is easy to find. And so is the MAD of this average: it is simply MAD/SQRT(9), according to the formula above. In this case, then, it is MAD/3. According to the table of test values, only 1 % of actual values are more than four MADs above the average, and the average error should be zero. The one percent test value for the average of the nine errors is then

$$\text{test value} = 4*\text{MAD of average errors} = 4*\text{MADAN}$$
$$= 4*\text{MAD}/3$$
$$= 1.333*\text{MAD}.$$

Suppose the MAD is 24. If the average error is 50, then something is wrong. The average error should be much less than 24 because of canceling; in fact, it should be larger than 1.333*24, or 32, only 1 % of the time. Thus there is a 99 % chance that the large average error is the result of an inappropriate model rather than of random variations, and a tracking signal trip should occur. In this example, it probably should have occurred much earlier.

Variation for Smoothed Errors

In the statistical analysis of the average error carried out above, the averaging was introduced when each error was multiplied by 1/N. The value of a smoothed error is a weighted average, which is found by multiplying each value by a different weight. For the last value, the weight is H; for the second, it is $H*B = H*(1 - H)$, for the third, it is H*B-squared, and so on. In symbols, the weight is WI, where $W0 = 1$, $W1 = B$, $W2 = H*B^2$, $W3 = H*B^3, \ldots, WN = H*B^N$. The weights therefore decrease in size as the process goes on. By applying the weight W1 to the most recent error, W2 to the previous error, and so on, the significance of older data is successively discounted. As was pointed out in the original discussion of weighted averages, this amounts to multiplying each value by a different fraction rather than multiplying them all by 1/N.

This kind of averaging, then, can be introduced into the argument above by multiplying each error by WI rather than by 1/N. Since WI (the weight) is different for each value of I (the position in the series), the arithmetic becomes a bit more complicated. For example, if there are two errors to be averaged, the weighted values of the MAD are W1∗MAD and W2∗MAD. The corresponding standard deviations are 1.25∗W1∗MAD and 1.25∗W2∗MAD, and the corresponding variances are $(1.25∗W1∗MAD)^2$ and $(1.25∗W2∗MAD)^2$. The sum of the variances is then $(W1^2 + W2^2)∗$ $(1.25∗MAD)^2$, and the square root of the sum, giving the standard deviation of the weighted average, is $1.25∗MAD∗SQRT(W1^2 + W2^2)$. This can be converted to a MAD by dividing by 1.25, with the result that the MAD of the smoothed error is $MAD∗SQRT(W1^2 + W2^2)$.

If more than two errors are to be used, of course, a longer series of additions and more weights are involved. Since all the weights are powers of B, the total can be simplified algebraically, but we will not go into the details here. They can be found in Brown* or worked out by ambitious souls. The result, as with the MAD of the average error, is a MAD which can be used in the 4∗MAD test value, or any other test value chosen from a table.

Change of Time Period

Business records are often kept in daily, weekly, or monthly form but used in terms of a different time period. Purchasing leadtimes supply one of the most common examples. A manufacturer or wholesaler needs to have an accurate estimate of sales variability in the period between the time he orders goods from his suppliers and the time they arrive. From this he can calculate a reasonable upper sales limit, and place his orders while he still has enough reserve stock on hand to cover that limit.

Of course, the leadtime period is not likely to be exactly a week or a month, and it is likely to be different for different suppliers. So the purchasing officer would really like to have a method by which he can *measure* variability on a monthly basis, the way sales figures are normally kept, but *use* it on a leadtime basis. The rule for combining variabilities provides the method. Suppose the leadtime is two months; sales in the leadtime are therefore the sum of the two monthly sales figures. The variability is known: it is simply the MAD. So the variability of the sum is SQRT(2)∗MAD, which equals 1.4∗MAD—if we assume that sales in one month do not influence sales in the next; that is, if we assume no autocorrelation. In general, according to our rule, the variability in a leadtime M months long would be SQRT(M)∗ MAD.

This is a good beginning rule, but in practice somewhat more accuracy can be achieved. This is because autocorrelation usually exists. Sales in

---

* *Ibid.*

one time period are usually related to sales in adjacent time periods. If this relationship is direct rather than inverse—that is, if high sales in one period are associated with high sales in the next, rather than with low ones—the net effect is to increase the leadtime sales variability. This increase can be reflected by increasing the value of the exponent used in combining the monthly figures. Taking the square root is equivalent to using the exponent $\frac{1}{2}$: $SQRT(M) = M^{1/2}$. The exponent can thus be varied fractionally to reflect the situation; when the exponent is 1, the variability is directly proportional to the leadtime. Figure 8–7 shows the effect of using various higher exponents.

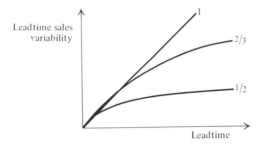

Fig. 8–7 Leadtime sales variability when different exponents are used. The exponent $\frac{1}{2}$ is used if there is no autocorrelation; the leadtime variability is then the square root of the leadtime value times MAD. Autocorrelation calls for a higher exponent and consequent higher leadtime variability.

To estimate the appropriate exponent in a specific situation, the following steps may be applied:

1. Find sales in successive two-month, three-month, four-month, ..., N-month periods.
2. Average all the N-month sales figures.
3. Find the logarithms of these averages, and of the numbers 1 through N.
4. Fit a straight line through these logarithms, using log N for the x-value and the log of the average for the y-value. The line will have a slope equal to the appropriate exponent.

This procedure need not be carried out for every item; if the items are reasonably similar a sample will suffice. If different items have radically different amounts of autocorrelation, of course, a separate analysis should be done for each, and a different exponent used. This is rarely necessary, however.

Stocks and Portfolios: A Useful Example of Combining Variability

The price of an individual stock traded on a major exchange fluctuates from day to day and even from hour to hour. Typical investors, both individuals and institutions, own shares of more than one company. Each stock varies in a different way from the others. Can statistical forecasting methods enable us to deal with the variability of a portfolio of different stocks, given the statistical facts about each stock in the portfolio? The answer is that they can, and that they can be very useful. This is because there is a relationship between the variability of a stock's price and the profitability of owning that stock. On the average, with many individual exceptions, highly variable stocks are more profitable to own than the more stable issues. This has been confirmed by decades of statistical work with stock price histories. The references list some of this work, and some evaluations and discussions of it.

Assuming this relationship between variability and profitability, how does the rule for combining variabilities come into play? Very directly: If you own more than one stock, the variability of the total portfolio is less, on a percentage basis, than it is if you own only one. Extending the idea, a diversified portfolio containing many stocks will be less variable than a concentrated one.

Suppose that an investor is willing to accept a certain level of variability in his portfolio's value, but no more. Limiting the variability also limits the profitability. But if this investor can diversify his holdings so that the total variabilities cancel out to some extent, he can maintain the same variability level overall but actually own individual stocks that are more variable, and thus more profitable. In other words, an investor can maintain a given variability level but gain more profit if he makes use of the rule for combining variabilities. Alternatively, he can reduce the variability of his investments without reducing earnings. This approach is so interesting that computer programs are available to analyze a given portfolio for the variability of each stock, and then to recommend other stocks that would increase profitability without increasing variability. The procedure is actually fairly complex, for a variety of reasons.

For instance, there is a great deal of correlation among the prices of various stocks. Early in this book a market average and prices of a typical stock were graphed together, showing high correlation. This means that the simple rule for combining the variabilities of uncorrelated data can't be applied without modification. It also means that the amount of reduction in variability which results from combining stocks is less than might be expected. But even with these restrictions the technique can produce some improvement, and is worth trying.

Exhaustive discussions and evaluations of this technique are available in the literature. If you intend to pursue them, one point of terminology is worth noting. Some authors, including Plotkin and Conrad, use the word "risk" instead of "variability." This emphasizes the psychological association between variability and risk in its usual sense of "risk of loss," but the meaning is simply "variability."

THE FAR EDGE OF UNCERTAINTY

Throughout this book we have naturally assumed that you have some reasonable amount of material on which to base your forecasts, no matter how much you may have to manipulate the data to make them usable. Now, however, we will approach briefly two cases where you have very little to guide you: when you must forecast from a very small number of observations, or when you are forecasting far into the future. The subject is covered in texts of statistical theory, and is generally of more use to the statistician than to the ordinary computer user; this section is only intended to serve as an introduction, emphasizing the ideas that may be important in practice.

Correcting for Few Observations

If you have a small number of observations of a normal variable, you can view their average as being itself a random variable. Therefore, as we have shown, you can calculate its variability, and from that a maximum or minimum likely value. You take the average (or mean) and add a variability measure, usually a fixed multiple of the MAD. But if the mean itself has substantial variability, which it does because you have few data points, you must also add a factor to account for it. The extra variability is referred to as "sampling error" (see Fig. 8–8).

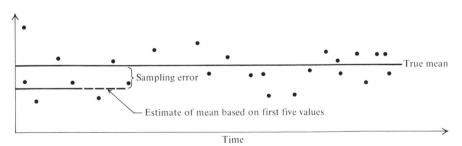

Fig. 8–8 Use of few data points adds a bit to the MAD, the amount of the sampling error.

Much work has gone into this problem, which is, as you can imagine, a common one, and statisticians have isolated a factor which can be used to correct the estimated standard deviation. The formula is $1/\sqrt{N}$, where N is the number of data points. This quantity is the standard deviation of the population of means based on different selections of N points.

In practice you will almost never have to use this factor; the MAD is based on the differences between forecasts and actual values, and therefore includes the major portion of all errors to be expected. Compared to this, the effect of variability caused by using few data is very small. There are only two real effects:

1. The standard deviation is somewhat less than 1.25*MAD if few data points are used; or, looking at it the other way, the MAD is slightly larger when there are few data points than when there are many (assuming the underlying process is the same).

2. Forecast accuracy can be expected to improve as more data points are accumulated. Statistical forecasters take advantage of this fact by using a relatively large smoothing constant for the first several periods in a new forecasting situation.

Forecasting Further Ahead

It is only when forecasts are based on forecasts that this increased variability can get you into trouble. This happens when a trend line is extrapolated further into the future, or a ratio is multiplied by itself to produce successive forecasts. Then the error introduced by using few data points grows larger.

You cannot eliminate this error, except by accumulating more data, but you can estimate how large it may be, which is the next best thing. Then instead of saying blindly, "Suppose the trend is off by ten percent . . . ," you can take into account the number of data points you have and actually calculate the possible sampling error (Fig. 8–9). The calculated sampling error then gives you a range, much like a confidence band, within which you can reasonably expect the true trend to lie—if the underlying process doesn't change. And there's the rub. Processes are always changing, especially in the very situations for which you have few data. The soap that sold 300 cases in its first test-market month may suddenly turn out to have an odor housewives dislike, or may alternatively catch on and outsell your stock. The Midwest may totally accept, or totally reject, your Australian beer after its first few cautious buys. With results like this always possible, even fore-casting itself may seem foolhardy, and a guess at the size of long-term error is probably every bit as good as a calculation. But at least now you will know enough to know what the statiscians are talking about, and to know that elegant formulas and precise terminology don't guarantee appropriateness. For most forecasting needs, the methods described earlier in this book are hard to improve on in practice. They *can* be improved on in theory; that's precisely why you can't leave forecasting to the staticians. And that is one of the major premises of the next section, on developing effective forecasting systems in practice.

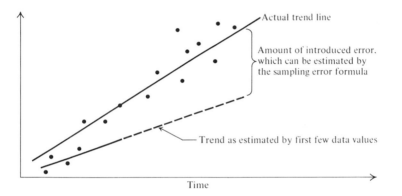

Fig. 8–9 Sampling error has relatively little importance unless you are extrapolating trends or ratios, so that the introduced error grows at each step. The statistician's estimate of sampling error can then be a useful indicator of the likely size of this introduced error.

PART 5 | MAKING IT WORK

CHAPTER 9

MAKING FORECASTING SYSTEMS WORK

The preceding sections of this book have explained a variety of forecasting techniques for use in marketing, production, investment and venture analysis, and government planning. But the way in which these methods are used is as important to successful forecasting as the methods themselves—in fact, it is actually more important, in a real, measurable sense. An appropriate forecasting method will in general produce a decrease in forecasting errors of from 10% to 50% if it is used properly. The same method, if it is used improperly, will produce an improvement of precisely zero, or even a worsening of the situation.

Almost all of the problems involved in using forecasting systems are people problems. The influence of technical details is much smaller than the influence of such factors as purpose, communication, agreement, and other human values.

Communications in Market Forecasting

The methods explained in this book can be applied very effectively to sales data, for example, once the actual sales processes in a given company or product group have been analyzed. The resulting forecasts are generally quite believable. But professional marketing people, product managers or their equivalents, also make believable sales forecasts. After all, it is part of their profession. In a typical company, the statistical forecasts are produced by a computer that is not operated or controlled by the marketing department, and the forecasting system that the computer uses has been produced by people unconnected with the marketing function. As a result, the marketing department is often reluctant to accept the statistical forecasts.

In fact, since the statistical forecasts are frequently lower than the marketing department's sales forecasts, bitter words and hard feelings often result from attempts to use statistical forecasts in overall management of the company. The marketing manager objects: not only are the forecasts produced by a computer that he doesn't understand or trust, but the lower forecasts seem to imply criticism of his own capability to sell. Perhaps the marketing people's higher forecasts reflect the optimism necessary for successful salesmanship; perhaps it is a reflection of the marketing man's tendency to dwell on the positive rather than the negative. Whatever the reason, the statistical forecasts often seem to the marketing man not only to be foreign, but also to be seriously *wrong*.

The technical specialists in turn retort that the marketing man has no recognizable method, no scientific justification at all for his predictions. This may be quite true, and experience does show that statistical forecasts are generally more accurate than those made by marketing people. The example shown in Chapter 4, where marketing managers for medical products consistently overestimated the effects of both their own and their competitor's actions and therefore produced widely fluctuating forecasts, could be repeated for a dozen industries. But calling names does no good, especially when the names themselves ("simulation results!", "no chi-square test!", "significance level—null hypothesis!") are in a foreign jargon that can only inflame passions further.

What Can You Do?

This failure of communication in the marketing area is typical, and situations like this present a severe problem. The sales manager is generally sincere about his forecasts. If he is right and the statistical forecasts are wrong, as he expects, then sales will be higher than the forecasts indicate. But production may be based on the statistical forecasts. If his expectations are correct, then, he will sell more items than the company makes—or, worse, he won't be able to sell them, because he can't deliver, even though the market is eager for them. Either way, the marketing man will suffer; and even if his expectations are proven wrong, and the statistical forecasts are the right ones, his worry in the meantime is bound to have repercussions.

The difference between the forecasts is also a problem for top management. What if they are convinced that the statistical forecasts are right, but the marketing manager insists on using his own forecasts? Then they may manufacture more than they can sell, and that will cost a great deal. It will have an especially obvious effect on the company's balance sheet: management looks rather ridiculous when sales go up but, due to overproduction, profits go down.

Somehow, the two forecasts must be reconciled. The first step in solving the problem is to communicate: the marketing manager should produce a forecast, and so should the statistical forecaster, and each group should know what the other forecasts. It is disastrous to plan production on the basis of statistical forecasts of sales *without* telling the marketing man what was done. When this approach is tried, the most likely outcome is that after a year or two management *will* tell the marketing man what is going on, but that it will be a different marketing man—the first one having quit.

The communication serves a number of purposes. First, it enables the marketing man to object. This makes him feel better, since he is no longer left out, and it also sometimes does turn up important facts which were not available to the computer. Second, and more important, it gives the marketing man a standard. He may tell management he thinks sales will be higher than the computer forecasts, but he will have to say *why*. And if he can't give a good reason for overruling the computer, he will be more apt to live with the statistical forecast, or at least to compromise with it.

One large drug manufacturing firm uses a variation of this system in deciding what new laboratory developments it should produce. A relatively simple computer program has been written for a timesharing terminal which sits in the room during annual product planning sessions. Both research executives and sales executives are present at these meetings. The computer program asks the research people for development cost, development time, and production cost estimates; it asks the marketing people for selling price, market size, market share, and the like. It then computes a simple profitability forecast based on these figures, and presents it to the group as a basis for discussion.

The key thing in this process is that the forecast is a basis for discussion. Plans and suggestions may now be based on some actual sales and profitability estimates, rather than on "gut feelings."

A large Western manufacturer of baked goods used a similar approach to setting sales quotas for its various divisions. A fairly straightforward timesharing program has been written to forecast sales for each division, based on past sales figures. At semiannual sales-planning meetings, the managers of all the divisions discuss the forecasts with top management. Managers, of course, have their own ideas about what their sales targets should be; however optimistic they may be in planning, they dislike being given specific quotas to fill. At this company, in the past, managers with high quotas were sometimes angry at management and bitter at other managers who had lower quotas. There happened to be good reasons for those lower quotas, but the rest of the managers only saw the figures and not the reasons behind them. Sometimes, of course, there were also genuine injustices. The semiannual discussion of the statistical forecasts has been in use for about two years now, and the results have been excellent.   The computer-generated forecast, because it is impersonal, has actually become a tool for better communication: all the facts on which it is based are open for discussion.   This would be worthwhile even if the procedure did not improve the forecasts themselves, although it did that as well.

DESIGNING AND DEVELOPING A FORECASTING SYSTEM

At least three principles should be kept in mind when a forecasting system is being developed:

1. Cooperation is better than opposition.
2. Tests are better than theories.
3. Simple systems work best.

These principles are applicable to most business and government systems, so what is said about them in the following pages applies to a lot more than forecasting.   But somehow it is easy to forget them when you are dealing with forecasts, because of the difference between the statistics and mathematics used in forecasting and the more mundane operations of most management data processing.   The mystical feeling that dealing with the future arouses in some people also comes into play, and sometimes leads forecasting system developers to act like omniscient "experts" rather than offering their help.

1. Cooperation

The designer of a forecasting system can regard himself as a salesman.   He has a variety of forecasting models in his sample kit; the organization of which he is part has a range of needs for forecasting and related services. The salesman's job, in the words that appear on Kaiser Corporation's cement trucks, is to "Find a need and fill it."   Some salesmen, it is true, try to force their product upon prospects who don't need it; but they are seldom highly successful, especially when their product is much more expensive and complicated than a scrub brush or a magazine subscription.

The most successful salesmen engage in "consultative selling."   Instead of spreading his wares and waiting for the prospect to pick, or telling the prospect why he should buy, the consultative salesman tries to find out just what the prospect needs.   Once the prospect has stated a need, the salesman has only to show how one of his products will fill that need.   He will often walk away with a signed purchase order from a prospect who had no intention of buying.

This is especially true in technical areas, most obviously because the customer seldom really knows what the product does or how it works, much less how it can help him. The statistician, computer specialist, or management scientist who is charged with developing a forecasting system in a typical established commercial or government organization is faced with a "market" of lower- and middle-management people who are not technical specialists. If these people are to help in developing the system—and they must, if it is to be appropriate—and later to use it, the technical specialist must make very clear just what he is doing and why.

But psychological factors are even more important than technical understanding. Middle management is often more than a bit suspicious of bright young men and women who, they feel, are trying to tell them how to do their jobs. They will often resent and resist. If the system designer simply explains his methods and what they do, he will probably just increase this resistance. But if he listens first, inquires about his "market's" problems and sincerely tries to understand, he can turn hostile forces into allies. Even if his ultimate system doesn't solve all problems—and no system can—or contains features that individuals don't like, they will remember that he tried, and they may even come to him with additional problems to be solved. Independent consultants say that the true test of their effectiveness is not what happens in a given study but whether or not they get repeat business; the same is true of internal consultants.

The practical details of cooperative system development call for:

1. Interviews. Talk to everybody—or, rather, listen to everybody.

2. Memoranda. Write down what a person says he could use, and send the memorandum back to him, in draft form, before you show it to anyone else. Your interviewee can then confirm that you understood him correctly, and that he meant to say what he did. This lets the interviewee know that you take him seriously, and also provides a written record which will help prevent disagreements later.

Let your market know whenever they raise a problem or make a suggestion which fits into one of your forecasting methods. Make them feel that they have a hand in developing the system, and make sure that is the truth, for your own sake as much as for theirs. They may well provide you with information or opportunities not otherwise available. In short, do it *with* your "market" rather than *to* them.

An excellent example of the kind of interviewing and reporting involved in cooperative system development is contained in R. G. Brown's *Decision*

Rules for Inventory Management.* The book is a collection of typical memoranda produced during development of an inventory control system. Only part of the work deals with forecasting, but the method, which is the important thing here, is very clearly illustrated.

2. Testing

Interviewing and note-taking will help convince people that you want to help them, but many may not yet agree that your system will in fact solve the problems you've been talking about. In other words, people may still ask, "But does it work?" Naturally you will be asking that question too, and the way to answer it is through tests and sample forecasts. Small tests using recent historical data should be carried out from the beginning. These are as important for system development as for public relations, and should generally include tests of alternate methods so that they can be compared for accuracy and ease of use. If you were planning on a moving-average system, for instance, but one based on exponential smoothing might be easier to use in practice, you would be wise to collect some data and test both methods. Even if you still decide in favor of the original plan, you will then have evidence with which to defend your choice.

When small tests like this are being carried out, it is often helpful to write a computer program to do the actual calculations. A statistician who has had a few hours of introductory instruction in computer programming should be able to produce the results of a simple test in an hour or so. The advantages of doing it by computer rather than by hand are the usual ones: arithmetic errors are eliminated, the results are printed legibly, it is easy to produce minor variations with almost no additional effort, and the writing of the program gives the statistician an opportunity to think through the logic of the forecasting procedure. This last is especially important, since the logic, once it is developed, will be used in ongoing operations "forever." It must be reviewed and reconsidered at every step of the development process, until the forecaster and his various "markets" all agree that it is right.

Throughout this book we have emphasized that the only measure of a forecasting system's worth is the accuracy of the forecasts. This leads to some general rules for testing, and one very important technical point: *the system must be tested against data which were not used in developing it.*

---

* Holt, Rinehart, and Winston, New York, 1967.

Suppose, for instance, that you have a year's worth of data. If you fit a trend line through all of it, and then start at month six to do forecasting and updating, the results will be meaningless. To be significant, the forecasts must be developed from only a portion of the data, and another portion, such as the last six months, must be reserved as "unknown" future data to be compared with the test results.

The concept of keeping test data separate from development data does not apply solely to time series forecasting, either. The two can get mixed together in almost any number of bizarre ways. For example, a group once spent several months developing a multiple-regression system to predict which applicants for personal loans would be bad risks. They selected more than 20 characteristics from the loan application file: marital status, length of time in present job, age, and so on. They collected data on these characteristics for a large sample of case histories, developed the regression program for them, and were then ready to test the results. They collected an entirely new data sample and processed it two different ways: first by means of the computer program, and then by having human clerks sort the cases into "good" and "bad" risks according to specific criteria.

The test procedure itself was obviously impeccable. And when the results came out, the group was elated: two of the factors showed extremely high correlation with the human evaluations. Then the group looked at what the two factors were, and their chagrin was classic. The two factors, "number of days delinquent" and "number of payments delinquent," were the same two the human clerks had used to sort the histories into "good" and "bad"— and they were precisely the factors that could not possibly be known before the loan was made.

In other words, the group had made the answer to their question into part of the procedure for asking it. Such incidents can only be prevented by keeping firmly in mind that the information you are trying to predict, whether it is next month's sales or a loan applicant's delinquency potential, must be absolutely unknown to the system.

Another implication of using the accuracy of the forecasts as the ultimate test of a system is that the goodness-of-fit measures used to fit trends, seasonal curves, and other forecasting patterns are *not* a proper guide to choosing the one to use in forecasting. A more complex curve, a trend line compared to a simple average, for instance, can always be made to fit the data more closely, simply because there are more ways to modify it to make it do so. But that does not mean that it will actually produce better forecasts.

In fact, if a model fits the development data too closely, it will probably produce bad forecasts, because it has been adjusted too carefully to a specific pattern of random variation that will not occur again. A dress manufacturer does not cut his patterns to fit exactly the contours of one specific woman, however flattering that exact fit might be to her. Instead he cuts with more leeway, to fit the wide variety of women who, despite their slightly different shapes, all wear size 9 or size 14. Simple forecasting models work best for many reasons, most of them human: they are easier to understand and hence less likely to develop obscure errors; errors are more readily apparent and easier to fix; the machine procedures are faster, less confusing to run, and probably less expensive. But there is also a statistical reason to prefer simpler models: the simpler the model, the more leeway it has built into it, and the more likely it is to produce reasonable forecasts in a variety of circumstances.

To some extent these comments are a repetition of those made on simulation as a tool for determining whether trends and seasonality are present. If the tests show that using trends produces more accurate forecasts, then a trend model is appropriate. A sample simulation will probably lead to the same conclusions as a trend test, but it may show up more clearly the cases in which the trend is so slight as to be not worth using. Moreover, doing a sample simulation gives you an excellent communication aid. Non-technical people may not understand the purpose or meaning of the trend test, but they *will* understand graphs of "what would have happened if we had used this method last year."

Large-Scale Tests and Data Problems

Small tests of methods can help you in communicating what you're doing as well as in choosing the right technique. Large-scale tests are also essential for evaluating the system, when it has been designed and sufficient data collected —but they should be done *quietly*. If the results of the first big tests are publicized, you may lose all the trust and goodwill you've been working for. Why? Because bugs, glitches, and other assorted wildlife tend to lurk unsuspected in programs and data until a really big test is run. These programming and data errors do not invalidate the system, but they may make your first forecasts wildly inaccurate.

For example, an inventory forecasting system was developed for a large manufacturer, and worked very well for a few typical items in the initial tests. A magnetic tape file of usages for the last two years was then developed, for all of the 50,000 items in stock, and the forecasting system was given its first big test with all the data. The results showed fantastically low forecasts for over half the items. Inspecting a few of the problem items showed the reason: they had been in use for less than two years.

The statistician on the project had intended his formulas to apply only to actual usage data: if an item had been in use for eight months, only the last eight values should be used to calculate the forecast. But the programmer, who was not a statistician, had misunderstood. There was a real programming difficulty, it turned out, in distinguishing between months in which usage was zero and zeroes which were due to nonexistence of the item. No file of "added-to-inventory" dates was available for items added within the last two years, although provision had been made in the new system for gathering this information on items added subsequently. So a compromise was struck: forecasting began with the earliest nonzero value, although there might be valid zero-usages before that.

But that was not the end of the problem. Another large-scale test was run with the corrected procedure, and most of the resulting forecasts looked all right. A few, however, were obviously too large. Investigation this time showed that the problem lay in returns to inventory, which had been recorded incorrectly. Instead of subtracting items which were issued and then returned unused, the data collection people had added them to the usage total. When there was a return, then, the magnetic tape file showed two usages when there should have been none, and consequently the totals for some items were overly large. The uncritical forecasting system then obligingly produced overly large forecasts for those items.

The most important fact about this example is that the problems encountered in the larger tests were predominantly data problems rather than forecasting model problems. In this project, which was part of a larger inventory control system that took two years to develop, the major delays and expenditures of effort were caused by the difficulties of accumulating and correcting data. This is typical of real forecasting projects, as opposed to academic ones, and both management and forecasting people should be well aware of the fact. It would not be too strong to suggest that the first day of a typical forecasting project should dwell on models and processes, but that the next month should be primarily devoted to collecting and verifying historical data.

3. Simplicity

One of the fortunate effects of the kind of continual testing of alternate methods mentioned above is that simpler approaches often turn out to be best. For instance, even in a situation where trends in data are present, the no-trend model may turn out to be more accurate than the trend model. This was the case, for instance, in an industrial operation where there was high variability in the usage of different materials because of changes in production schedules. Some items did have trends, but the variability influenced the trend calculations to such an extent that a simple exponential smoothing model was more accurate than a trend model. Conceivably, some third model—perhaps one involving trend tests—would have been more accurate than either, but of the systems that were tried, the simplest one turned out to be best, even for some items which very clearly had trends.

Another example of this situation was discussed earlier, in connection with seasonality. There the method of general exponential smoothing using sine curves was introduced. When data have much variability, this very elegant and appealing method is simply less accurate than the more prosaic seasonal index method.

Some psychological facts are involved in this situation as well. People dealing with their own organizations are very closely attuned to minor changes in the way things are going. To the people involved, these minor changes often seem like truly major ones, and the people overreact. As we noted, this is probably the reason for the relative inaccuracy of sales forecasts made by marketing people. They know that a big promotion is under way, for example, and expect sales to go up. Sales *do* go up, but not as much as the marketing man expects. Perhaps it is because his expectation is partly a hope rather than a cold calculation of probabilities.

This is connected to simplicity in models because in constructing a model, the forecaster naturally wants to reflect all the processes that affect future values. If there are promotions, the forecaster wants to insert a promotion input into his model which will increase the forecast to some extent. If there is seasonality, the forecaster is naturally tempted to use the seasonal-index model instead of the simpler trend model. But sometimes including these factors costs more than it gains.

The solution to these problems is to test alternate systems. If the use of promotions in forecasting improves forecasts, keep the more complex model. If not, simplify. Of course, data on hand may be too limited to enable you to test this or other possibilities. In that case, the solution has to be delayed a little: this aspect of forecasting systems is discussed in the next section.

DEALING WITH LITTLE INFORMATION

We have described several technical means of getting started when there is inadequate historical information, but these did not take into account the public-relations factor. You want to keep people informed, give them results as soon as possible, and reassure them that you take them seriously and are interested in their concerns. There are two methods for doing this, one emphasizing what you're going to get, and one using what you're getting right now. Either or both, added to the technical procedures, should help you achieve your public-relations goals.

Feedback

Suppose you are designing a forecasting system for a medium-sized manufacturing firm. The sales manager tells you, "Promotions have a tremendous effect on sales—when I try to predict, the first thing I look at is the promotion budget and schedule." The production manager has told you, "I don't notice promotions. I know when we have 'em, but I don't see any particular effect on the plant orders."

Almost no historical data are available except monthly sales figures. Promotions last about two weeks, are frequent, and sometimes overlap, and no record has been kept of promotional expenditures, except for the annual budget. You have two general strategies available in designing your forecasting system:

1. You can try to get the production and marketing people to come to an agreement, and use the result in your system.
2. You can design into your system a procedure for measuring promotional efforts and keeping track of sales thereafter, to tell you as time goes by what promotions actually do.

Obviously, alternative two is the preferable one. A guess or compromise can be used to start the system off, and future information can then be used to correct the guess as time passes and experience builds up. (How might you compute the updated parameters? Exponential smoothing? Correct!) This requires putting the effects in quantitative terms. For instance, you might ask the sales manager, "How many dollars of additional sales do you think you get for each dollar spent on promotions, on the average?" Suppose he guesses, "Two." Then your forecasting system might be given provision for recording promotional expenditures as they occur. It can react by distributing an amount of sales equal to twice the expenditure over the succeeding weeks.

How should it be distributed? Does half the addition come in the first week of the promotion, perhaps? Or does 90% of it come in the first week?

There's really no way to be sure except to gather information. Once again, you can start off with a guess from the marketing people, but the system should be designed to collect actual data and correct the guess you have made.

The effect of the promotion is, from a technical viewpoint, the difference between actual sales and the forecast which you make *without* including the promotion factor. Your system should keep track of this difference, and use it in two ways:

1. It should update the promotion forecasting effect parameters. Suppose on the average the difference between nonpromotional forecast and actual promoted sales in the first promotion after you go into operation is four times the cost of the promotion. The promotion multiplier, originally 2.0, should be increased, possibly by exponential smoothing, and perhaps using a high factor like 0.2 instead of the usual 0.1 or 0.05. The result is a new factor of 2.8 times the promotional expense.

2. The results should be displayed on management reports: not the before-and-after parameter values, but rather the nonpromotional forecast, promotional forecast, and actual result. If there have been a series of promotions, a group of them and some summary totals should be shown. This gives management facts which may surprise them.

Information Reporting

The second approach, that of emphasizing the information gathered for use in forecasting rather than the actual forecasting use of it, is often useful. For instance, in the very complex simulation of the residential housing in San Francisco discussed in Chapter 2, the very complexity of the model led to lack of understanding and, more important, lack of acceptance of the results. Presentation of intermediate information, such as lists of undervalued or overvalued houses, might have been helpful. This could have been done in a very simple form for the city planning staff, in a way that would be clear to them. Had this sort of thing been built into the system, acceptance would probably have been better. And, of course, this comment is closely connected with the first recommendation in this chapter, that system development be done *with* the users rather than *to* them. This is still true if the users seem to be unsophisticated to the system designer. A very sophisticated system which is never used is a far worse product than a simple one that the users like. It is even worth sacrificing a bit of accuracy to achieve this, although such sacrifice is hardly ever necessary.

The Dollar Value of Forecast Errors

While simple, understandable systems often turn out to be the most useful, there are some exceptions. Two kinds of feedback, in particular, can be very useful to the technical people who are responsible for forecasting. Information on the *causes* of forecast errors can obviously help them to improve the system. More surprisingly, information on the potential *dollar value* of improvements in the forecasting method can also be valuable. This may not tell them what they should do to improve the forecasts, but it may tell them whether it is worth doing anything at all.

The causes of forecast errors can often be seen in pictorial representations of the errors. A simple graph of errors, or of the smoothed error, kept over a long period, may reveal that errors tend to be positive, so that forecasts underestimate actual events, or negative, so that they overestimate. An even more useful concept has been used in several figures earlier in this book; it is the graph of forecast changes against actual changes. Graphs like this can reveal systematic over- or underestimation of changes, or inability to forecast the direction of change consistently. The graphs are drawn with a central line showing where all the points would fall if the forecasts were perfect; the key to interpreting these graphs lies in comparing the actual positions to this "line of perfect forecasts."

Numerical techniques can also be used to supplement the graphs. Each type of error has its own measurement formula; a report can show the forecaster how much of his overall error is due to systematic overestimation, how much to underestimation, and how much to the inability to recognize changes. A periodic report of these measurements to the forecasting staff can be very useful, assuming that the staff understands the significance of the measurements. This topic is a fairly technical statistical matter; details can be found in Henri Theil's *Applied Economic Forecasting.**

Similarly, the dollar value of forecast accuracy may be a fairly technical quantity to calculate. Sometimes it is fairly straightforward. For example, in the most common inventory control systems, such as those described by Brown and by Magee and Boodman in the books listed in the bibliography, the amount of inventory which must be held to assure customers a desired level of service depends partly on the average forecast error. In these systems the forecast error, measured by MAD, is multiplied by a safety factor chosen by management, and that amount of stock is held to guard against forecast errors. The dollar value of safety stock is easy to find: it is simply the unit price of the item multiplied by the number of units in the safety stock.

---

* Rand-McNally, Chicago, 1966.

Obviously if the forecasts can be made more accurate the MAD will decrease, and a dollar value of the resulting decrease in safety stock can be found. Figure 9–1 shows some ficticious but quite plausible numbers to illustrate the concept.

Value of inventory	$1,000,000
Percent safety stock	20%
Value of safety stock	$ 200,000
Average forecast error (MAD)	20%
MAD if forecast errors could be reduced 50%	10%
Resulting safety stock	$ 100,000
Dollar reduction	$ 100,000
Annual value of this dollar reduction	$10,000–$20,000 depending on investment opportunities

Fig. 9–1 Sample calculation of the dollar value of increased forecast accuracy in an inventory control system. Safety stock is directly proportional to the Mean Absolute Deviation, which is essentially equal to the average forecast error.

Once again, more complicated situations may call for more complicated analyses of the dollar cost of forecast errors. For instance, in many situations which involve regression analysis, the forecaster is able to control one or another of the variables which influence his dependent variable. In business, investment influences profit. In the public sector, government expenditure influences the GNP. In each case, the forecaster may have a target value: so much increase in profit or in GNP. But, to complicate matters, he may also have a target value for the variable or variables under his own control. He may wish to invest just so much in inventories or in public works. Now the "error" can be interpreted as the sum of two different deviations—the deviation of the forecast from the preferred value of the dependent variable, and the deviation of the controllable variable from the preferred variable. When you add the variability due to forecast error into this, you can get an estimate of the dollar cost of the forecast errors. Once again, details can be found in Theil; his discussion is concerned mostly with national economics.

In any case, when people with the right kind of technical background are involved in a forecasting system, some of the more sophisticated technical methods can turn out to be useful. As always, the danger is that use of the sophisticated concepts by people who don't really understand them will hurt more than it helps. Only the largest organizations find genuine use for the more technical concepts, but any organization should be aware that forecast errors cost money and that that cost can sometimes be measured, and any forecaster should give thought to methods of identifying the important sources of error in his forecasts.

THE EFFECTS OF COMPUTERS

Just as computers have had a tremendous effect on the way ordinary business operations are carried out, they have had a strong influence on *what* is done in forecasting and on *how* it is done. Contrary to the impression held by a great many people who do not have computer experience, the major influence of computers in the business world has *not* been to replace clerical workers with monster machines. In fact, the rather extensive evidence which has been produced by commercial research firms and by students of business administration, usually in doctoral theses, tends to support the idea that after computerization there are slightly more clerical workers involved than otherwise.

Instead, the main effect has been to vastly increase the productivity of a staff of clerical workers. It has often been pointed out, for example, that if telephone service had continued to depend on manual exchanges the entire female population of the United States would have become totally engaged in manning telephone exchanges long before the present level of telephone communication was reached. The effect of computerizing or mechanizing telephone exchanges has not been to throw telephone operators out of work; instead, the main effect has been to vastly increase the amount of service provided by a steadily growing corps of operators.

Similarly, in the paperwork associated with business operations, the computer has very rarely caused more than temporary adjustment in work-force size. Instead, the computer has enabled businesses to provide detailed billing to their customers, to accurately control their inventories, to compute payroll deductions and the like on a scale never before possible. Useful work is done which otherwise simply would not be done, and the number of workers involved is either the same or larger.

In forecasting, too, the computer has enabled a greater deal of additional useful work to be accomplished at no increase in either work force or cost. Since the computer can do a great deal of complicated arithmetic, it has reduced the need for statistical clerks specially skilled in arithmetic, although at the expense of an increased need for computer programmers, another type of specialist. (Actually the same people are probably involved: the two skills require the same sort of temperament.)

The main effects of computerization on forecasting in business, industry, and government have been as follows:

1. The amount of computation which can be involved in a forecasting procedure is now virtually unlimited. The manager or forecaster has been liberated from restraints posed by human educational limitations, human errors, and the speed (or lack of speed) of mechanical calculators. For instance, in the past it was almost impossible to use on a practical basis forecasting procedures which involved square roots. Multiplications were dangerous enough, given human error frequencies and the difficulty of hiring staff capable of doing this kind of work.

2. The amount of data which can be used in developing a forecast has become similarly unrestricted. A computer can maintain files containing sometimes hundreds of past data points for a given inventory item, plot of land, city population, or whatever the forecaster is dealing with. In the past this has not been the case, since early computers were restricted by their input speed and it was important to restrict the files to one or two computer cards. However, with the advent of tapes and disk storage devices these restrictions have been removed; the forecaster can now plan to make use of all the data available to him, and usually wishes for more.

It is worth noting in this context that the amount of arithmetic a computer can do is much larger than the amount of reading and writing it can do. In the time it takes to read one number from a tape file, a computer can do many hundreds of complex calculations. The limitation on data has thus not entirely disappeared. And some limitation on computational complexity is still imposed by the inability of programmers to develop computations beyond a certain level of complexity within a reasonable time. This is a real limitation, since every computation used in a forecasting computer must be programmed by a skilled and valuable professional. But these limits are small compared to the overall effect, and your audience, the people to whom you present those dazzling and manifold pages of printout, will probably never be aware of them.

3. The fact that to use a computer a set of instructions must be prepared by a programmer, who is a scarce and highly paid resource person, means that the forecasting routines actually used in conjunction with computers are only the most important ones, ones where the forecasting problem is important enough to justify the investment of a programmer's time. On the other hand, once a forecasting routine has been completed, it is very easy and quite inexpensive in most cases to use it as often as may be desired. For

this reason, one of the main influences of computerization on forecasting has been to encourage the development of *repetitive* routines for forecasting.

For many business operations, forecasting must be done periodically. For instance, manufacturers generally need to forecast requirements for raw materials supplies and repair parts for their machinery monthly. Tax assessors and other public officials need to forecast biannually and sometimes quarterly. In the past, limitations on human resources, both in numbers and in working speed, meant that only the most important forecasts could be revised as frequently as might be desirable. For instance, a wholesaler might investigate his high profit lines on a weekly basis, but review less important items only annually. These shortcomings were necessary when human labor was the only way to get the job done, but once computer routines had been developed, they could be used to eliminate this shortcoming. In fact, much of this book has dealt with effective methods of revising forecasts on a routine, periodic basis. The new methods, in conjunction with computers, have had the same net effects on forecasting as mechanization has had on telephone exchanges. We can do a lot more at the same cost.

The technological developments which have made the computer such an important force in management today will in all probability continue to expand. More important than new inventions which enable computers to do more things, however, will be the continuing series of inventions which reduce the costs of computers. Computers themselves already represent only about one-third of the cost of computerization; two-thirds of the cost lies in programmers, operators, managers, and supplies. The trend will probably continue, and the net effect will be cheaper computers and more computer power for everyone.

The Future of Forecasting

As these trends in computer costs continue, two major results are likely to affect forecasting:

1. As the cost of programming a new system rises, while machine cost decreases, and as the quality of available computer programs increases, there will be more use of existing packages and less reprogramming of forecasting methods.

2. As experience accumulates and costs drop, simulation models for use both in evaluating new ventures and in managing existing ones will become more common.

Prepared computer programs intended for use by several purchasers are usually called *packages*. There have long been computer packages available for doing some of the traditional statistical analyses associated with forecasting, notably regression and correlation analysis. One or two packages for exponential smoothing and for updating have also been developed and sold. However, these programs intended for routine use have not been very successful. The main reasons have been: first, insufficient testing, and second, lack of flexibility.

Lack of testing has meant that small errors have remained in the packages even after years of use, so that incorrect forecasts resulted. In one exponential smoothing system examined by the author, updating of a trend was done by using the value $X - F$ as the "true" trend. Of course, the value $(X(T) - X(T - 1))$ should be used. The result of this error, which essentially said that the trend was too low whenever the forecast F was lower than the actual value X, was to introduce cyclical errors into the forecasts. But the system was several years old, and this bug wasn't discovered until after the package had been in use for several months in this particular installation.

But as packages like this one are used for longer periods in wider varieties of problem situations, the number of undiscovered bugs should approach zero. And many minor but helpful refinements can be expected to be incorporated. The resulting systems should be very satisfactory. They should be even easier to use, and cheaper to install and test, than custom-made forecasting routines, just as an auto from Detroit is easier and cheaper to obtain than an equivalent custom-made vehicle.

Here is an example of the kind of refinement that will make packages helpful. We have emphasized the need to compare alternate forecasting methods by using a simulation or test run of the forecasts, and to compare forecast accuracy of alternate models rather than other attributes (such as comprehensiveness, mathematical elegance, or stylishness). Writing a computer program that incorporates all likely models for a given situation is a large job in itself; adding a program which compares the results of several of these makes the job a major one. But most computer packages enable the user to test at least the level, trend, and seasonal-model accuracy, and sometimes also to attempt to use regression or correlation methods.

Once these systems are refined and proven, it will be easier to learn to use one, and to adapt one's forecasting system to a good package, than to develop one's own. The rapidly increasing cost of programming will accelerate this trend.

This trend toward use of packaged programs is related to the second influence of the trends in computer and programming costs.   Overall corporate performance is related to several variables: labor costs, material costs, sales rate, taxes.   Management as a whole is more interested in overall effects than in minor adjustment of production runs and the like.   But as more complex forecasting methods are developed, tested, and accepted, they will be used for increasingly complex management tasks.   The new venture simulation presented at the beginning of this book is an excellent example of this sort of development.   That example was a new venture being contemplated by a group of entrepreneurs, but the same method can be applied even more effectively to planning decisions in large, existing organizations.

Once a forecasting model of an organization has been developed to tell management what will happen in the future, given the facts about today's costs and sales, it can be used to play the "what if" game.   In the new venture analysis example, the questions to be answered were of the form, "What if we hire more salesmen?" and "What if we hire fewer salesmen?"

In an existing firm, the questions might be, "What if we build a new distribution center on the West (or East) Coast?" or, "What will the overall effects of the unions' wage requests be, if they are accepted?" or, "What effect on profits will the new tax law have?" These analysis questions are partly forecasting questions, but they are structural forecasting problems rather than simple statistical ones.   As computer programs are developed which embody structures useful to many different organizations, this type of forecasting system will become more common—and more important.

The questions that these systems can be used to deal with tend to be larger questions, concerned with major investments or policies.   In a word, they are *planning* questions, concerning top management, whereas the changes in sales rate for one product, or the trend in usage of manufacturing supplies, are of concern to lower management levels and have to do with *control* of on-going programs, rather than with planning for new ones.

The overall effect of computers in forecasting in the future will thus be expansion from forecasting for control to forecasting for planning.   This movement will be reflected in the increasingly important role of structural models; development efforts will be concentrated on corporate models and other planning simulations. The routine forecasting and updating for control purposes will increasingly be performed by standard, well-tested packages.

This change will bring forecasting closer to other disciplines in management science. For instance, simulation has already been linked with statistical forecasting in this book, and further connection with corporate modeling is suggested above. These subjects are in turn connected with operations research, which is largely the technique of designing mathematical models of business and government operations. So the methods discussed in this book can be expected to develop further and to be even more useful in the future than they have been in the past.

BIBLIOGRAPHY

Modeling and Operations Research

Benton, W. K., *The Use of the Computer in Planning*, Addison-Wesley, Reading, 1971. Written at the same level as this book, emphasizing actual experience rather than theory.

Brewer, Garry D., *Evaluation and Innovation in Urban Research*, RAND Corp., Santa Monica, Aug. 1970. Publication number P4446.

————, *Mastering the Complexity of Urban Decision: Integration of the Computer*, unpublished Ph.D. Thesis, Yale University, Department of Political Science, 1970.

Brown, Robert G., *Management Decision for Production Operations*, Dryden Press, Hinsdale, Ill., 1971.

Hillier, Frederick S., and Gerald J. Lieberman, *Introduction to Operations Research*, Holden–Day, San Francisco, 1967. An introduction for mathematicians or engineers, more technical than this book.

Morse, Philip M., and Laura W. Bacon (eds.), *Operations Research for Public Systems*, MIT, Cambridge, 1967. Paperback; several case histories are discussed at about the level of this book.

Theil, Henri, *Applied Economic Forecasting*, Rand-McNally, Chicago, 1966. A more theoretical development of regression techniques for national economics, with some very practical applications and methods.

Statistical Analysis

Alder, Henry L., and Edward B. Roessler, *Introduction to Probability and Statistics*, W. H. Freeman, San Francisco, 1962. An introduction to useful mathematics and statistics, one level more technical than this book and clearly written.

Draper, N. R., and H. Smith, *Applied Regression Analysis*, John Wiley & Sons, New York, 1966. Gives a technical but fairly clear discussion of the various procedures involved in using regression.

Miller, Irwin W., *A Primer on Statistics, for Business and Economics*, Random House, New York, 1968. Written simply and for nontechnical people. Short. Exceptionally clear explanation of regression and other concepts.

Time-Series Forecasting

Brown, R. G., *Statistical Forecasting for Inventory Control*, McGraw-Hill, New York, 1959. Written for an intelligent but not necessarily technical person. Contains a bibliography.

————, *Smoothing, Forecasting, and Prediction of Discrete Time Series*, Prentice-Hall, Englewood Cliffs, 1962. A theoretical development, for mathematicians. Contains a bibliography.

Gumbel, Emil J., *Statistics of Extremes*, Columbia University Press, New York, 1958. Fairly technical, but contains material not found in most statistics texts.

The Stock Market

Conrad, Gordon R., and Irving H. Plotkin, "Risk/Return: U.S. Industry Pattern," *Harvard Business Review* **46,** No. 2 (March–April 1968), pp. 90–99.

Cootner, Paul H. (ed.), *The Random Character of Stock Market Prices*, M.I.T. Press, Cambridge, 1964. Interesting; contains articles written at various technical levels.

Fisher, L., "Outcomes for 'Random' Investments in Common Stocks Listed on the New York Stock Exchanges," *The Journal of Business* **38,** No. 2 (April 1965), pp. 149–161. Also many other articles in other issues of *The Journal of Business*.

Markowitz, Harry M., *Portfolio Selection: Efficient Diversification of Investments*, Wiley, New York, 1959.

Mazuy, Kay K., and Jack L. Treynor, "Can Mutual Funds Outguess the Market?" *Harvard Business Review* **44,** No. 4 (July–August 1966), p. 113ff.

Inventory Control

Magee, John R., and David M. Boodman, *Production Planning and Inventory Control*, 2nd ed., McGraw-Hill, New York, 1967. This or one of the similar books is necessary reading if you are going to apply forecasting to inventory control.

INDEX

INDEX